D1741739

Vineyard Visits

PETER JANSSEN

HarperCollins*Publishers*

National Library of New Zealand Cataloguing-in-Publication Data

Janssen, Peter, 1953-
Vineyard visits : 150 of New Zealand's best / Peter Janssen.
ISBN 978-1-86950-666-7
1. Wineries—New Zealand—Guidebooks. 2. Vineyards—New
Zealand—Guidebooks. 3. Wine districts—New Zealand—
Guidebooks. I. Title.
641.220993—dc 22

First published 2007
HarperCollins*Publishers (New Zealand) Limited*
P.O. Box 1, Shortland Street, Auckland

Copyright © Peter Janssen 2007

Peter Janssen asserts the moral right to be identified as the author of this work.

All rights reserved. No part of this publication may be reproduced,
stored in a retrieval system or transmitted in any form or by any
means, electronic, mechanical, photocopying, recording or otherwise,
without the prior written permission of the publishers.

ISBN-13: 978 1 86950 666 7
ISBN-10: 1 86950 666 9

Cover design by Sarah Bull, Anthony Bushelle Graphics
Typesetting by IslandBridge

Printed by Everbest on 128 gsm Matt Art

*To all those 'wise women of the world' who have saved
me from making innumerable foolish decisions.
You know who you are!*

Acknowledgements

Many thanks to all the very hospitable folk at vineyards up and down the country. Your enthusiasm and friendliness are a credit to your industry.

Special thanks to the fine editorial team at HarperCollins — Lorain Day, Eva Chan and Teresa McIntyre — for all their patience and professional advice and help.

Thanks to Mike, Steve and Michelle, Warren, Richard and Neil for putting up with me.

Peter Janssen
June 2007

Contents

Introduction

Before undertaking this book, while I drank wine as a drink of choice, my knowledge of wine and the wine industry was minimal. Like most consumers I purchased my wine in a supermarket, venturing into more specialist stores from time to time for a special occasion. To be *very* honest, the label design probably influenced me more than the contents. However, like so many people I also enjoy the vineyard experience, and the focus of this book is as much on what New Zealand's excellent vineyards have to offer as on sampling and drinking wine.

While there are now over 500 vineyards in New Zealand, many are contract growers without any winemaking facilities, while others are not open to the public or are open only by appointment. Nor does this book include every vineyard open to the public, as the choice becomes too bewildering for the average visitor. Instead I have put together a selection that I feel covers the broadest spectrum of vineyards, from tiny boutique wineries to large commercial establishments complete with restaurants, gift shops and accommodation. Exclusion of any vineyard certainly is not intended to imply lesser quality of wine.

The explosion of vineyards has brought with it an expanding wine-tourist industry, and the good news is that most vineyards open to the public have retained that natural friendliness for which New Zealand is internationally famous. The wine industry sometimes has a reputation of being somewhat pretentious, but this is very rarely reflected by the people on the front line, and even more rarely by winemakers. To enjoy your vineyard experience simply ask questions, no matter how simple and basic, and you will find vineyard folk full of enthusiasm and information — all freely given without condescension.

Tasting

Tasting is generally free in New Zealand for individuals, though there is often a charge for groups (usually 10+). However, a number of wineries do charge and this has been indicated in the book. While the general public assumption is that wine tasting should be free, spare a thought for the wine producer who supplies knowledgeable staff, clean glasses and premises, and has to pay tax on the wine supplied free of charge. Also, if you are paying for the tasting you are free to taste at leisure without any obligation to buy.

Winery and vineyard tours

In these days of regulation, most vineyards have neither the staff nor the facilities to offer tours, although for a handful a winery tour is part of their business. However, many smaller wineries are happy to show visitors around their premises, particularly if they are not busy. If you want to look around, just ask.

Accommodation

Many wineries now offer accommodation, and this has been indicated in the book. They range from bed-and-breakfast-type arrangements through to luxurious apartments and lodges.

Hours

While the middle- and larger-sized vineyards have regular hours, many of the smaller owner-operated business have more irregular hours. While I have tried to be accurate at the time of printing, it would not hurt to phone ahead to double-check opening hours, especially around harvest time (March to May) and in winter.

Winery cafés and restaurants

For many if not most people, one of the most delightful experiences is vineyard dining. Almost without exception the food focus is on good-quality fresh local produce, and New Zealand's vineyard eateries are among the country's best. However, this can come at a price, and it pays to check the winery's website before sending your credit card into shock! In every area there are vineyards that have superb picnic facilities, and in fine weather this is a good and affordable alternative to eating in.

Bottle sizes

The Bible has plenty to say on wine, and for some reason the Old Testament has been a rich source of names for the larger bottles of wine. Bottle sizes are as follows:

Quarter bottle	187 ml	(champagne only)
Half bottle	375 ml	
Bottle	750 ml	
Magnum	1.5 L	(2 bottles)
Double magnum	3.0 L	(4 bottles)
Jeroboam	4.5 L	(6 bottles)
Imperial	6.0 L	(8 bottles)
Salmanazar	9.0 L	(12 bottles)
Balthazar	12.0 L	(16 bottles)
Nebuchadnezzar	15.0 L	(20 bottles)

The entrance to this winery is rather unprepossessing. The Chambourcin grapes along the drive look uncared for, but are in fact a variety that have light leaf growth; and, as Ake Ake does not use herbicides, the grass amongst the vines is often long. In addition the exterior of the small cellar and restaurant is rather plain and the garden planting still new. But step inside and the true nature of Ake Ake is revealed. Small, modern and very smart, the bottle-lined walls and dark, polished wood give this winery an instant warm appeal that is at once both welcoming and stylish.

As Northland's newest winery, Ake Ake has at this stage only a small vintage of Syrah, Chambourcin and Pinot Gris with Tempranillo due in the near future. What makes Ake Ake particularly interesting is that it also offers a hand-picked selection of around 100 wines from small New Zealand vineyards and select international vintages. These wines can be purchased to accompany meals. There is a vineyard tour each day at 11.30 at no charge.

The intimate restaurant is vegetarian with some seafood (vegan options also available), and Ake Ake takes great pride in preparing meals from fresh food and in offering a wide selection of wines suitable for vegetarians and vegans.

Ake Ake Vineyard

165 Waimate North Road Kerikeri

Labels Ake Ake

Specialisation Syrah
Chambourcin

Opening hours
Wed–Sun 10 am–6 pm
Dinner Thurs–Sun
Closed July

Tasting No charge
Phone 09 401 7137
Website www.akeakevineyard.co.nz

Cottle Hill Winery

**Cottle Hill Road
Off State Highway 10
Kerikeri**

Labels Cottle Hill

Specialisation Pinot Noir
Chardonnay
Pinot Noir Rosé
Syrah
White port

Opening hours
Nov–Apr
Daily 10 am–5.30 pm
May–Oct
Wed–Sun only

Tasting **$5, refunded on any
purchase**

Phone **09 407 5203**

Website **www.cottlehill.co.nz**

Barbara and Mike Webb are serious about wine and aim to provide visitors to their winery with more than just a casual tasting in the relaxed atmosphere of their pleasant vineyard just outside Kerikeri. Cottle Hill staff are more than pleased to adapt the tasting experience to individual tastes across a broad range of wines from an unusual white port to Pinot Noir and Chardonnay. The winery also produces grappa, a powerfully strong spirit (90% proof) of which only the 'heart' of the distillation process is kept for sale. Now producing 36,000 bottles a year, Cottle Hill's wines include Chardonnay, Sauvignon Blanc, Pinot Noir Rosé, Cabernet Sauvignon, Cabernet Merlot, Merlot, Pinot Noir, Syrah, Muscat, and tawny and white port.

Arriving in New Zealand from San Diego in their 10-metre yacht *Sprig*, the family settled on a lovely property with a long, westerly-facing slope with views out to the Puketi Forest where fresh café-style food can be enjoyed while overlooking the vineyard. Cottle Hill Winery is about having a winery experience where you can come and learn, and enjoy the lifestyle.

New Zealand's most northerly vineyard, Karikari Estate is set high on the slopes above Great Exhibition Bay and has an openness that is attractive in its own right and takes full advantage of the superb views. On a bright sunny day, the vista from the winery is dazzling, looking far north toward the cape and the white sands of Parengarenga, across to Houhora Harbour and Mt Camel, and below to 500 hectares of wetlands and the wide sweep of Karikari Beach.

Part of the Carrington resort, the vineyard was planted on the upper slopes to take advantage of the breeze which helps lower the humidity, though the site is naturally fairly dry and surprisingly good for growing grapes. The range is also surprising with the estate planted out in Chardonnay, Viognier, Semillon, Syrah, Cabernet Sauvignon, Merlot, Malbec, Cabernet Franc, Pinotage and Montepulciano.

The modern winery is partially set into the hillside to aid in keeping the vintage cool, and in addition to wine tasting, Karikari Estate also offers wine tours and light meals. Information regarding accommodation and the golf course is available on the website.

Karikari Estate

Maitai Bay Road
Karikari Peninsula, Kaitaia

Labels **Karikari**
Silver Bay

Specialisation **Chardonnay**
Pinotage

Opening hours
Daily 11 am–4 pm

Tasting **$10**
Phone **09 408 7222**
Website **www.karikariestate.co.nz**

Marsden Estate

Wiroa Road, Kerikeri

Labels Marsden

Specialisation Chardonnay
Syrah

Opening hours
Aug–May
  Daily 10 am–5 pm
June/July
  Daily 10 am–4 pm

Restaurant Fri/Sat evenings all year

Tasting Casual visitors no charge,
groups small charge

Phone 09 407 9398

Website
www.marsdenestate.co.nz

Established in 1993, the winery takes its name from Samuel Marsden, an early missionary who planted the first vines in New Zealand. Set in the lush countryside just out of Kerikeri amid orchards of oranges and olive groves, this four-hectare vineyard produces single-estate wines including Pinot Gris, Chardonnay, Syrah, Chambourcin and Pinotage, with Sauvignon Blanc grapes brought in from Marlborough.

Popular with both locals and visitors alike, the restaurant and winery are an attractive country-inn-style building designed by local architect Martin Evans. The Mediterranean-influenced menu suits the relaxed dining atmosphere both on a beautiful, wide terrace overhung with grape vines in the summer, and indoors in a warm, open room complete with a cosy open fire in winter. The view is over a lily pond to the vineyard on the gentle slopes beyond.

There is something immediately incongruous about mixing palm trees and grape vines, but at Okahu Estate the two do grow together and it's a very appealing combination.

Vines were first planted here in 1984 on the slopes above the sea, and now this winery produces a wide range of wines including Pinotage, Cabernet Franc, Malbec, Merlot, Chardonnay and Viognier. Okahu won New Zealand's first gold medal for Syrah way back in 1996, long before this grape became popular and at a time when the ruling wisdom was that New Zealand, let alone Northland, could not produce good red wine.

In addition to wine tasting, the small cellar offers local produce for sale and there is also vineyard accommodation.

Okahu Estate

520 Okahu Road
Kaitaia

Labels **Okahu**
       Shipwreck Bay

Specialisation **Syrah**
       Chardonnay
       Chambourcin

Opening hours
Dec–Feb
  Daily 10 am–5 pm
Rest of year
  Mon–Fri 10 am–5 pm

Tasting **Casual visitors no charge, groups small charge**

Phone **09 408 2006**

Website **www.okahuestate.co.nz**

✳ Omata Estate

Aucks Road, Russell

Labels **Omata**

Specialisation **Syrah**
Chardonnay
Merlot

Opening hours
Lunch/dinner
Dec–Mar daily
Rest of year Wed–Sat
Wine tasting
Same days from 10.30 am

Tasting **$5 per person**
Phone **09 403 8007**
Website **www.omata.co.nz**

While not the easiest place to get to, the superb site of this boutique vineyard overlooking the Bay of Islands is well worth the effort. From the restaurant, rows of grape vines roll down the hillside towards the blue waters of the bay glistening in the distance during the day, while at night the lights of Paihia sparkle in the distance.

Syrah, Chardonnay and Merlot are grown on the land at Russell, with Sauvignon Blanc grapes brought in from Marlborough to supplement the range. The grapes are all hand-picked and the wines are single estate with no blending; Omata vintages are available only from Omata and selected restaurants.

The restaurant is superb (with prices to match, so check the website for details). Huge, weathered, wooden beams complement the warmth of the old brick floor and wide windows open out on to a terrace with expansive views of the bay beyond. An open fire adds warmth on a chilly winter's evening. The kitchen itself is open to the dining area and only the finest and freshest food is prepared there. A grape arbour is no mere decoration – when ripe the grapes are used to make a Syrah jus for selected dishes.

In addition, the vineyard is in a 'kiwi zone', and you might just hear the call of New Zealand's national bird while dining here on a warm summer's evening.

Reserve

A term used to imply that the wine is of a higher quality than usual; occasionally used too 'freely'.

This extremely popular vineyard is undoubtedly one of the highlights of the Matakana wine-growing area and an ideal day-trip from Auckland. Not only does Ascension produce 16 varieties of wine, but the stylish vineyard restaurant (opened in 2000) has maintained both its food quality and its charm over the years. The atmosphere is relaxed and friendly with tile floors and wooden ceilings creating a natural warmth, with spacious indoor dining opening through wide doors to terrace dining complete with an outdoor fireplace. The focus is on fresh New Zealand produce prepared with a Mediterranean influence, and matched with wines which can be tasted at the table.

In addition to Merlot, Malbec, Pinotage and Chardonnay grown on the steep slopes at Matakana, Ascension also sources Riesling, Gewürztraminer and Sauvignon Blanc from Gisborne and Marlborough. Ascension was one of the first vineyards to plant Viognier back in 1996, and an unusual Californian variety known as Flora was planted in 1997 under the impression that it was Pinot Gris; it is now bottled under the name of 'The Rogue'. Owners Darryl and Bridget Soljan are the latest of five generations of winemaking tracing back to early Dalmatian immigrants and West Auckland vintners.

Expanded recently to include a wedding and conference centre venue with an enormous stained-glass window of the wedding feast at Cana, Ascension now caters for over 50,000 visitors a year yet still maintains a friendly family atmosphere. In addition to wine tasting and the restaurant, the winery hosts small concerts and also offers a wide range of gift items and condiments.

Ascension Vineyard

480 Matakana Road Matakana

Labels **Ascension**

Specialisation **Chardonnay Viognier**

Opening hours
Daily 10 am–5 pm
Lunch 11 am–4 pm
Dinner Thurs/Fri/Sat 6.30 pm on

Tasting **$8 per person; includes an Ascension glass to keep**

Phone **09 422 9601**

Website
www.ascensionvineyard.co.nz

Simon Devitt Glass House

Brick Bay

Arabelle Lane
Snells Beach

Labels Brick Bay

Specialisation Pinot Gris
                Cabernet
                Sauvignon Franc
                Pharos

Opening hours
Daily 10 am–5 pm

Tasting $4 per person, refundable
         on purchase

Phone 09 425 4690

Website www.brickbay.co.nz

Nestled in a steep-sided valley behind Snells Beach, this small winery only opened to the public in early 2007, though the vineyard had already produced 10 vintages. The heart of this vineyard is the immensely stylish 'Glasshouse', designed by Auckland architect Noel Lane. Almost totally made from glass with warm wooden floors of Tasmanian oak, this building houses the tasting room and straddles the edge of a large pond on which modern waterborne sculptures drift in the breeze amongst the water lilies.

In addition to Pinot Gris, Brick Bay produces a fine Bordeaux-style blend under the name Pharos, and olive oil which is also available for tasting.

In the bush-lined valley, the winery has also established a sculpture garden, a winding trail leading through the trees and featuring an outdoor gallery of works by some of New Zealand's leading artists (there is a $10 fee for entry to the sculpture garden and the works are for sale).

Heron's Flight has a reputation for its Italian-style red wines and is the only vineyard in the country to grow Sangiovese and Dolcetto. It also has a reputation for good food in a relaxed setting, and many regulars were anxious that in moving from the old rambling café to the modern restaurant building, Heron's Flight would lose some of its rustic charm. Never fear. While the new building is, well, new, attention to detail in the construction and landscaping will ensure that the new building will be as much-loved as the old. Loosely based on the New Zealand villa, and around sustainable principles in its design and construction (e.g. it is solar-powered), the restaurant looks out over the lush Matakana countryside to the bush-clad slopes of Mt Tamahunga, and out to the Hauraki Gulf with Little Barrier Island in the distance. Beyond the wide terrace with its wood-fired pizza oven is a French-kitchen herb garden and a colonial vegetable garden including crops of unusual varieties of Maori potato. Inside the bistro the bar is complete with classical zinc top and a ceiling imaginatively created from old barrel stays, while the couches are covered in a unique material made from recycled plastic milk bottles.

All the wines are produced from the six-hectare property surrounding the winery and are only available locally. In addition Heron's Flight also sells wine from selected small vineyards plus condiments made in its kitchen under the Flights of Fancy label.

Heron's Flight

49 Sharp Road, Matakana

Labels **Heron's Flight**

Specialisation **Sangiovese**
Dolcetto

Opening hours
Daily 8.30–evening

Tasting **$10 for three wines**

Phone **09 422 7915**

Website **www.heronsflight.co.nz**

Hyperion Wines

Tongue Farm Road
Matakana

Labels **Hyperion**

Specialisation **Bordeaux-style wines**

Opening hours
**Sat/Sun/public holidays
    10 am–5 pm
27 Dec–6 Feb
    Daily 10 am–5 pm**

Tasting **$5 per person;
        groups by appointment**

Phone **09 422 9375**

Website
www.hyperion-wines.co.nz

Hyperion Wines takes its name from the mythological Greek god Hyperion, an early sun god and father of Helios (the sun), Selene (the moon) and Eos (the dawn). In keeping with this classical theme all Hyperion wines are named for Greek gods. Here on just 2.4 hectares Hyperion produces six varieties, both red and white, in a rustic setting that is immediately appealing. The winery and tasting room are in an old cowshed, and alongside the shed the stainless-steel trailer of an ex-beer-tanker is used as supplemental wine storage. But there is nothing rustic about Hyperion's wines as they produce some very fine wine, especially their flagship Cabernet Sauvignon simply known as 'The Titan'. All the production processes are done in a traditional hand-crafted manner, right down to the use of cork in bottling. In addition to wine Hyperion also produce a grappa made in an old copper still.

Their wines are only available from the cellar door or through selected outlets in Matakana and Auckland.

This 'Californian Mission' style winery with its earth-colour tones is set in the middle of the largest vineyard in the area (16 hectares), producing Pinot Gris, Chardonnay and Syrah. In addition vineyards in Marlborough contribute Sauvignon Blanc, and from Hawke's Bay comes Merlot and Cabernet Franc. Peter Vegar, the current director, has a family connection with a long line of Dalamatian vintners beginning with Luka Lunjevich who arrived in New Zealand in the late nineteenth century.

From the winery the views are over the wide slopes of the vineyard to the hills behind Matakana, and visitors are encouraged to take a relaxed approach to wine tasting on the comfortable, warm, north-facing terrace.

Matakana was among the first vineyards to plant Pinot Gris, and it is fitting that this varietal has been its most successful wine.

Matakana Estate

568 Matakana Road
Matakana

Labels **Matakana Estate**

Specialisation **Pinot Gris**
Chardonnay
Syrah

Opening hours
Daily 10 am–5 pm

Tasting **$5 per person, refunded on purchase**

Phone **09 425 0494**

Email
cellar@matakanaestate.co.nz

Terroir

A French term loosely translated as 'a sense of place'. It is the sum of the effects of the local environment, such as soil and weather, on the resulting wine.

Omaha Bay Vineyard

189 Takatu Road
Matakana

Labels **Omaha Bay**

Specialisation **Pinot Gris**

Opening hours
Summer
 Daily 10.30 am–5 pm
Winter
 Daily 10.30 am–4 pm

Tasting **Three wines for $5,**
     eight wines for $10

Phone **09 423 0022**

Website **www.omahabay.co.nz**

Omaha Bay is a newly established boutique vineyard and was planted in 2002 with Pinot Gris, Syrah, Flora (a Gewürztraminer/Semillon cross), Montepulciano, Viognier, Malbec, Cabernet Franc and Petit Verdot. In addition to these grapes the winery also sources grapes from Hawke's Bay, Huapai and Marlborough, adding Chardonnay, Pinot Noir, Sauvignon Blanc and Merlot wines to its range.

With outstanding views over Omaha Bay, Little Barrier Island and the outer Hauraki Gulf, the winery offers platters of fresh local produce as well as wine tasting and sales.

Ransom Wines

46 Valerie Close
Off State Highway 1
Warkworth

Labels **Ransom**

Specialisation **Pinot Gris**
Dark Summit (a
Bordeaux-style
blend)
Chardonnay

Opening hours
Tues–Sun 10 am–5 pm
Daily Christmas to Waitangi Day

Tasting **$5 per person, refundable**
on purchase

Phone **09 425 8862**

Website **www.ransomwines.co.nz**

Established in 1993, Ransom Wines grows classic French varieties on this single seven-hectare, family-owned and -operated vineyard near Warkworth. Pinot Gris and Chardonnay plus the Bordeaux-blend varieties are all grown on the home block. In 2006, Ransom Wines discovered through DNA analysis that one of these was actually an ancient variety, Carmenère – it is the first winery in New Zealand to produce a wine bearing this label. An exciting Syrah from Matakana, Sauvignon Blanc from Marlborough, limoncello and grappa complete the line-up.

The small winery, designed by architect Graeme Scott, is an example of stylish New Zealand architecture, allowing views into the working part of the winery and capitalising on the rural vista. Open and airy, and often featuring original New Zealand art, Ransom is a lovely relaxed spot to taste wine or just enjoy a glass or two with platter lunch of local seasonal delicacies.

Artisan Wines

99 Parrs Cross Road Oratia

Labels **Artisan**

Specialisation **Chardonnay Syrah**

Opening hours
Daily 11 am–5 pm with extended summer hours

Tasting **$5, refunded on any purchase**

Phone **09 838 7979**

Website **www.artisanwines.co.nz**

The Sunde family has been growing grapes in the Oratia area for over 100 years. Representing a new generation of winemakers, Rex and Maria Sunde have created a delightful modern boutique winery in the heart of the 'old' West. After travelling through suburban Henderson, the drive into Artisan Wines reveals a bucolic lush and green valley with vines surrounding the small, stylish winery loosely based on the traditional New Zealand bach. Open and airy, Artisan offers wine tasting, platter food during the week, and a full lunch menu on weekends and public holidays. The Oratia vineyard produces Syrah, Chardonnay, Flora (a cross between Gewürztraminer and Semillon), Merlot and Cabernet Franc, while vineyards in Marlborough, Gisborne and Hawke's Bay provide grapes for Sauvignon Blanc, Pinot Gris, Pinot Noir, and Gewürztraminer. The wines are all single-vineyard vintages, and are only available from the vineyard and selected retail outlets — not supermarkets.

From summer 2007, a local farmers' market will operate alongside the winery on Saturdays. Just a few metres away is the Packing Shed Café and gallery and the fascinating curio shop Just Plane Interesting.

In 1910 Josip Babich, like many Croatians at the time, immigrated to the gumfields of Northland, but two years later, at the age of 16, he planted his first vineyard; and by 1916 had produced his first wines, thus beginning a 90-year association of the Babich family and wine in New Zealand. In 1919 the family moved to the property in Henderson which had been purchased earlier, and began planting vines. Today this small vineyard is surrounded by dense new housing subdivisions, but still produces Pinotage, Chardonnay and Pinot Noir, while grapes are brought in from Hawke's Bay and Marlborough to be processed at Henderson. The large, spacious winery overlooks the vineyard and is backed by an attractive garden; visitors are welcome to bring a picnic and taste the extensive range of wines.

Babich Wines

9 Babich Road
Henderson

Labels **Babich**

Specialisation **Sauvignon Blanc**
Pinot Gris
Merlot
Riesling

Opening hours
Mon–Fri 9 am–5 pm
Sat 10 am–5 pm

Tasting   **Casual visitors no charge,
groups small charge**

Phone   **09 833 7859**

Website **www.babichwines.co.nz**

Collard Brothers

303 Lincoln Road
Henderson

Labels **Collards**
Rothesay

Specialisation **Viognier**
Chardonnay
Merlot
Chenin

Opening hours
Mon–Sat 9 am–5 pm
Sun/public holidays 11 am–5 pm

Tasting **No charge, but not set up for formal tasting or specialist tourist services**

Phone **09 838 8341**

Email
collardsnzwines@xtra.co.nz

In an area dominated by Dalmatians, English horticulturist JW Collard founded this estate on Lincoln Road in 1910. For many years the Collards worked closely with their winemaking relatives and neighbours the Averill brothers, and the late Lionel Collard was well known for his unstinting enthusiasm for the New Zealand wine industry. Now, almost 100 years later, the company is still in family hands and run by brothers Bruce and Geoffrey Collard. While road widening has taken a toll on the Lincoln Road vineyard, this area still produces Merlot and Malbec supplementing grapes grown at the Collards' own Rothesay vineyard at Waimauku or brought in from Hawke's Bay and Marlborough. Collards was one of the first vineyards in New Zealand to grow the rising star of white varietals, Viognier.

This is a great spot to grab a good deal on case wines, including the option of mixed cases for those who like to try different types of wines.

Wine awards

To the outsider, the proliferation of wine awards can be confusing. The key awards for New Zealand wines are :

- Air New Zealand Wine Awards
- Royal Easter Show Wine Awards
- Liquorland Top 100
- Sydney International Top 100
- London International Wine Challenge

While the actual vines surrounding Lincoln have disappeared under housing developments, this winery has been operated by four generations of the Fredatovich family from Lincoln Road since 1937. Wine tasting is available in a modern, spacious facility across a wide range of wines made from grapes brought in from the Hawke's Bay and Marlborough. Lincoln specialities include its ice wine which requires the grapes to be frozen before the juice is extracted, mature port aged for at least 40 years, and a Chardonnay of consistent quality. There is a small picnic area alongside the winery, and Langtons, a function centre for larger occasions, is also located on the property.

Lincoln Vineyards

130 Lincoln Road Henderson

Labels **Lincoln**

Specialisation **Chardonnay**
Ice wine

Opening hours
Mon–Fri 9 am–5.30 pm
Sat 10 am–5 pm
Sun 12 noon–4 pm

Tasting **Casual visitors no charge, groups small charge**

Phone **09 838 6944**

Website **www.lincolnwines.co.nz**

Wine label information

Under food regulations, wines sold in New Zealand must identify the country of origin, the producer's name and address, alcohol strength (e.g. 12% alcohol by volume) and contents by volume (e.g. 750 ml). Wines given the name of a single variety must contain not less than 75% of the stated grape. Where two or more varieties are stated, the varieties together must constitute not less than 75% of the contents and be named in descending order of proportion. For example, for a wine labelled Cabernet Sauvignon/Merlot, the main grape will be Cabernet Sauvignon. New Zealand wine labels fall into two categories:

- varietals (e.g. Coopers Creek Riesling) – here the wine is named by the grape variety from which it is produced;

- branded (e.g. Esk Valley 'The Terraces') – here the wine is labelled and sold on the strength of its unique brand name, and the buyer will need some prior knowledge as to its contents or rely on the description on the back label.

Mazuran's Vineyard

255 Lincoln Road Henderson

Labels **Mazuran**

Specialisation **Port**

Opening hours
**Mon–Sat 9 am–6 pm
Sun 9 am–5 pm**

Tasting **No charge**
Phone **09 838 6945**
Website **www.mazurans.com**

When you arrive at Mazuran's Vineyard the first reaction is that you have accidentally swung into the wrong driveway. But continue down past the roses and the classic 1960s Mazuran home to a small doorway tucked into the side of what looks like a garage. This doorway leads to a wonderland of ports and sherries, the mainstay of the Mazuran vineyard since it was established in 1938. Equally surprising is that all these wines have been produced from a single vineyard behind the house. Producing quality port under a label unchanged for decades, this winery proudly has port for sale for every year since 1942! In addition, Mazuran's also claims to be the first New Zealand winery to send wine to an international competition, in 1956.

But this winery doesn't rest on yesteryear glory. Under the counter of the shop lined with wine maturing in oak barrels is a small glass case crammed with medals won; in 2005 Mazuran port was the only port in the world to take a double gold medal in the prestigious San Francisco International Wine Fair (including entries from Portugal, the original home of port). In addition the vineyard each year produces a single table wine of white (Moselle) and red (Cabernet Savignon/Merlot).

Like many of the other wine families in the area, the Mazurans are of Croatian origin; their wines are only available from this outlet.

Pleasant Valley Wines

Pleasant Valley Wines was established in 1902 by the Yelas family, who were among the first of many Croatians to establish vineyards in the Henderson area. Typical of those early vineyards, the Yelas family still live, grow grapes and process the harvest all on the one property, though now the local production of Pinotage is supplemented by grapes from Waiheke, Hawke's Bay and Marlborough. Originally, like most other vineyards in the area, the Yelas family mainly produced sherries and ports to cater for the unsophisticated New Zealand taste, and Pleasant Valley Wines today still produces these fortified wines along with both red and white table wines. The modest cellar is open for wine tasting and purchases.

322 Henderson Valley Road Henderson

Labels **Pleasant Valley**

Specialisation **Port**
　　　　　　 Chardonnay

_____

Opening hours
Mon–Fri 9 am–5.30 pm
Sat 11 am–4.30 pm
Sun 10 am–4.20 pm

Tasting **No charge**
Phone **09 838 8857**

Dalmatians

Dalmatians (more affectionally known as 'Dallies') immigrated to New Zealand from the Dalmatian coast of modern-day Croatia, which before World War I was part of the Austro-Hungarian Empire and for most of the twentieth century part of Yugoslavia. The original pioneers of the New Zealand wine industry were not Dalmatians but other immigrants, mainly (but not exclusively) from Europe, including Spain (Soler, Vidal), Germany (Wohnsiedler, Breidecker), Lebanon (Corban), Hungary (Kasza), Scotland (McKenzie), Italy (Bragato, Zame) and Russia

(Muaga). Many Dalmatian families arrived later through association with horticulture and the decline of the kauri gum fields in Northland. They settled predominately in west and northwest Auckland in the nineteenth and twentieth centuries, making this area the birthplace of the New Zealand commercial wine industry.

　Babich, Fredatovich, Yelas, Delegat, Brajkovich, Nobilo, Selak, Fistonich, Mazuran, Balich, Soljan and Yukich are just some of the many Dalmatian families that have made significant contributions to the New Zealand wine industry.

Sapich Brothers

**150 Forest Hill Road
Henderson**

Labels **Sapich**

Specialisation **Fortified wines
Purple Death**

_____

Opening hours
**Mon–Thurs 12 noon–6 pm
Fri/Sat 10 am–6 pm
Sun 1 pm–4 pm**

Tasting **No charge**

Phone **09 814 9902**

Website **www.sapich.co.nz**

_____

Arriving at the Sapich Brothers' winery is like stepping back into the 1960s and everything good that represents. Three generations of the Sapich family currently work at the winery, and in the tradition of 'Old West' Auckland it will always be a family member who serves the visitors in their small shop. Established in 1933, and covering 30 hectares, the winery produces an astounding range of wine. In addition to more modern styles of both red and white wine, Sapich has an incredible array of fortified wines that have long since disappeared elsewhere: cream sherries and ports of every kind, ginger wine, Blackberry Nip, apricot and cherry brandies and an especially delicious Old Cream Liqueur that has been matured in totara barrels for no less than 25 years. These wines have warmth and an alcohol content not found in modern table wines. One visitor suffering from decades of insomnia claimed that imbibing Sapich port had produced the best sleep in years, though no mention was made of the amount drunk to break this sleepless cycle.

This winery produces the famous Purple Death, a red-wine concoction in production since 1966 and which proudly claims on the label to be 'an unusual rough-as-guts aperitif that has the distinctive bouquet of horse shit and old tram tickets'.

This is a friendly place, the shop-cum-tasting-area is worn and cosy with the atmosphere of an old bar, and you are even welcome here in your gumboots! For those wanting a genuine 'Westie' experience of hospitable Dally winemaking, you can't go past the Sapich Brothers.

Residual sugar

Residual sugar refers to the amount of sugar remaining after fermentation has finished or has been artificially stopped. Sugar is measured in grams per litre.

Reached via a vine-flanked driveway, a wisteria-entangled doorway leads to a very pleasant tasting room at this large family-owned vineyard that has been operating in this area since 1980, and now produces over 130,000 cases of wine annually. While the vines around the winery produce Merlot and Pinot Gris, Coopers (like most other vineyards in Kumeu wine country) brings in grapes from Gisborne, Marlborough and Hawke's Bay to be processed at Huapai. The Coopers Creek Swamp Reserve Chardonnay is especially recommended.

In addition to wine tasting and sales, Coopers Creek has a superb picnic area overlooking the vineyard, complete with a grape-covered terrace, wood-fired barbecues, attractive gardens planted in New Zealand natives, a large lily pond, an outdoor chess set and a covered, outdoor, barrel-lined eating area. The area is spacious enough to hold large and small groups in several individual picnic areas; a cheese board is available; and wine is for sale by both the glass and the bottle. While there are no winery tours, the operations area is clearly visible from the public area.

In addition to live jazz on Sunday afternoons (January to Easter), Coopers Creek runs a number of events through the summer including Coopers Creek Wine Festival, Film in the Vines, Coopers Vineyard Jazz, Art in the Vineyard and the Scarecrow Festival (see the website for details).

Coopers Creek

601 State Highway 16 Huapai (just north of Kumeu)

Labels **Coopers Creek**

Specialisation **Chardonnay Riesling**

Opening hours
**Mon–Fri 9.30 am–5.30 pm
Sat/Sun/public holidays
10.30 am–5.30 pm**

Tasting **Casual visitors no charge, groups small charge**

Phone **09 412 8560**

Website **www.cooperscreek.co.nz**

Kumeu River Wines

550 State Highway 16 Kumeu

Labels **Kumeu River**

Specialisation **Chardonnay Pinot Gris**

Opening hours
Mon–Fri 9 am–5 pm
Sat 11 am–5 pm
Sun closed

Tasting **Casual visitors no charge, larger groups by appointment**

Phone **09 412 8415**

Website **www.kumeuriver.co.nz**

The most boutique of the Kumeu wineries, this vineyard has a reputation for outstanding quality across a range of just five wines: Chardonnay, Pinot Gris, Sauvignon Blanc, Merlot and Pinot Noir. Even more unusual is that 80% of the grapes for its wines come from Kumeu vineyards with only Sauvignon Blanc grapes coming in from Marlborough. A family-owned business, the vineyard was established by Mick Brajkovich in Kumeu in 1944 and his son Maté continued making wine under the San Marino label, which in 1986 became known as Kumeu River. Now a third generation of the Brajkovich family continues this strong viticultural tradition, reflected by a collection of fine historic photographs lining the walls of the small tasting room, including photos by renowned New Zealand photographer Marti Friedlander.

Chardonnay has been its strength in recent years and, while the range is small, Kumeu River offers the opportunity to taste across a wide range of vintages.

Harvesting

Grapes are harvested either mechanically or by hand. The decision to harvest is generally made by the winemaker and viticulturalist, and decided upon by the level of sugar (brix) and acid of the grapes as well as flavour, tannin levels and the weather.

Mechanical harvesting has the advantage of covering large areas of the vineyard quickly with a minimum labour investment. Wines made from grapes that benefit from quick harvest, such as Sauvignon Blanc, are almost always harvested mechanically. Hand-picking has the advantage of minimising damage to the grapes and also leaving behind grapes that have bunch rot, are not ripe, or have other defects.

At Matua Valley a tree-lined drive leads through grape vines to the winery with a pleasant outlook over the verdant wine country around Kumeu. The large cellar area offers wine tasting, wine sales and a selection of gourmet New Zealand foods and wine-related products. There are several small picnic areas near the winery including one with a children's playground, and below the winery is the pleasant 'lower field', an area ringed by mature trees and big enough to hold several large groups (complete with barbecue area), with plenty of room for a game of touch or cricket.

Established in 1973 by brothers Ross and Bill Spence, Matua Valley was the first to recognise the potential for Sauvignon Blanc, and today this is still a signature wine for it, along with Pinot Noir, Riesling and Pinot Gris. The 60-hectare home block around the winery produces a small amount for production, though most of the grapes come from company-owned vineyards in Gisborne, Hawke's Bay and Marlborough, producing a wide range of red and white wines under a variety of labels.

Next door to the winery, the legendary Hunting Lodge has a reputation as one of Auckland's finest restaurants (phone 09 411 8259).

Matua Valley

Waikoukou Road
Waimauku

Labels Ararimu
       Innovator
       Matheson
       Shingle Peak
       Matua Valley

Specialisation Sauvignon Blanc
          Pinot Noir
          Riesling
          Pinot Gris

Opening hours
Daily 10 am–5 pm
Closed Christmas Day, Boxing
  Day, Good Friday; and Anzac
  Day until 1 pm

Tasting Casual visitors no charge,
      larger groups small charge

Phone 09 411 8031

Website www.matua.co.nz

Nobilo Wines

**45 Station Road
Huapai**

Labels Nobilo
Bach 22
Castle Cliffs
Drylands
Fernleaf
Monkey Bay
Rose Tree Cottage
Selaks
Station Road
The Jibe
White Cloud

Specialisation Chardonnay
Sauvignon Blanc
Pinot Noir
Merlot
Riesling
Pinot Gris

The Croatian flag and colourful flowerbeds greet visitors to New Zealand's second-largest winemaking concern, Nobilo Wine Group. Established in the Kumeu area in the early '40s by the Nobilo family, this winery is in fact the oldest in this part of West Auckland, and now produces a huge range of wines catering for every taste under a plethora of wine labels. The shop and tasting room retains a cosy atmosphere with wood panelling, stained glass, an open fire in winter and a small shady picnic area. Here you can sample a range of 15 wines each day which includes Nobilo's Australian vintages. Tucked away in the corner is a fascinating cabinet displaying old bottles and wine labels from the 1950s and '60s, and some of the numerous medals won by Nobilo wines.

Pinotage is still grown on the land surrounding the winery, but the vast production of the Nobilo group comes from vineyards in Marlborough, Gisborne and Hawke's Bay to be processed at Kumeu, Hawke's Bay and Marlborough.

Opening hours
Daily 10 am–5 pm

Tasting Casual visitors no charge, larger groups small charge

Phone 09 412 6666

Website www.nobilowinegroup.com

Tony Gatman Photography

Soljans Estate

366 State Highway 16
Kumeu

Labels **Soljans**

Specialisation **Sparkling wines**
Sauvignon Blanc
Riesling
Pinotage

Opening hours
Daily 9 am–5.30 pm

Tasting **Casual visitors no charge, groups small charge**

Phone **09 412 5858**

Website **www.soljans.co.nz**

From the traditional Croatian greeting of 'Dobro Dosli' at the entrance to this large bustling winery, visitors will receive a warm welcome from the Soljan family who have been making wine in West Auckland since 1937. Relocated in 2002 from the urban sprawl of Lincoln Road, Henderson, the use of Hinuera stone on the Kumeu vineyard reflects the traditional Dalmatian stone buildings, while the large family-friendly café is a more human expression of the natural warmth of the Croatian people.

The vineyard around the winery grows Pinotage, Pinot Gris and Merlot grapes, but the bulk of the grapes comes from vineyards in Gisborne, Marlborough and Hawke's Bay to produce a range of white and red table wines under the single Soljan label. In addition to wine tasting, the café is open for breakfast and lunch, and Soljans can cater for special large occasions. The café with its Mediterranean-style menu also won the 2007 New Zealand Beef & Lamb Hallmark of Excellence Award and, reflecting the strong Croatian sense of family, the café has a children's menu and a play area just off the café terrace so parents can dine in peace while keeping an eye on their offspring.

The winery hosts the enormously popular Berba Festival over Easter weekend, a traditional Croatian harvest festival where visitors can help crush the harvest by foot, indulge in platters of Croatian food, and be entertained by Dalmatian music and dancing.

The atmosphere at Soljans is summed up by their own special rules for pétanque which begin: 'Players are not allowed on the pitch without a full glass of wine in their hand.'

West Brook Winery

215 Ararimu Valley Road Waimauku

Labels West Brook
        Blue Ridge

Specialisation Riesling
                Chardonnay
                Sauvignon Blanc
                Pinot Noir

Opening hours
Mon–Sat 10 am–5 pm
Sun/public holidays 11 am–5 pm

Phone 09 411 9924

Website www.westbrook.co.nz

While this vineyard was established in 1999, the Ivicevich family has been growing grapes and making wine in West Auckland since 1935, and like many other winemakers moved from the Henderson area as a result of the pressure of urban growth. The company takes its name from the West Brook area of Henderson where the family had their original vineyards. Still rather new, the winery has a large, pleasant picnic area with plenty of room to kick a ball around, a pétanque court, and an outdoor chess set. Tastings are available across a good selection of red and white wines, and large windows in the upstairs tasting room give an excellent view into the actual winemaking area and over the vineyards.

On the Sunday and Monday of Labour Weekend, West Brook hosts a Food, Wine and Music Festival in a large marquee in the spacious grounds.

A little tricky to find but worth the effort – the map under 'Contact us' on West Brook's website should help.

The stylish new winery at Cable Bay is a low-profile modern building, partially built into the hillside which emphasises its dramatic location with superb views over the inner Hauraki Gulf. The grand black-basalt entryway leads via a wide flight of steps to a foyer featuring New Zealand art, off which are the restaurant, bar and tasting room. A wall of glass along the entire side of the building facing the sea gives uninterrupted views of the vineyards and beyond that to Auckland city, while off the dining area, a small sheltered courtyard is an ideal spot for a glass of wine or a meal.

In addition to the vineyard surrounding the winery, Cable Bay has 10 other vineyards around the island, and further vineyards in Marlborough from which it produces Sauvignon Blanc and Pinot Noir. Traditional techniques are employed in the production of the wines, from hand-picking through to bunch-crushing, and a viewing gallery gives visitors an overview of the winery. The barrel hall lined with cool river stones is especially attractive, and in addition to wine Cable Bay also produces its own olive oil.

Cable Bay Vinyards

85 Church Bay Road Oneroa

Labels **Cable Bay**

Specialisation **Sauvignon Blanc Chardonnay Pinot Noir Bordeaux-style blends**

Opening hours
**Daily 11 am–5 pm
Lunch Tues–Sun 12 noon–3 pm
Dinner Wed–Sat from 6 pm**

Tasting **$5 per person**
Phone **09 372 5889**
Website
www.cablebayvineyards.co.nz

Wine blends

Some of the world's most famous wines are blends of different grapes (Bordeaux, Chianti, Châteauneuf du Pape, Côtes du Rhône). While it may be difficult at times to discern all the individual grape varieties, they all bring something to the mix. Blending of different varieties is only recommended when it is possible to marry qualities which complement each other. Certain varieties such as Pinot Noir, Riesling and Gewürztraminer are rarely blended with each other. Skilful blending by the winemaker can add new dimensions of weight, length, colour, style and complexity.

Cassito Miro Winery and Eating

3 Browns Road Onetangi

Labels **Miro**
       Archipelago

Specialisation **Bordeaux-style reds**
       Ratafia

Opening hours
Christmas–end Jan daily 11 am–4 pm
Feb–Easter Wed–Sun 11 am–4 pm
Closed Apr
May–Christmas Sat/Sun & Fri
  evening for dinner (reservations
  required)

Tasting **Charge varies according**
      to size of tasting glass
Phone **09 372 7854**
Website **www.mirovineyard.co.nz**

Accessed by a drive lined with pencil Italian cypress, Cassito Miro is a small vineyard set high above Onetangi on very steep and terraced land. Producing a very individual range of wine carefully watched over by an anxious woman, Cat and Barnett Bond only use grapes grown in their 2.5-hectare vineyard to produce Bordeaux-blend wines as well as Rosé and ratafia, a grape-based aperitif. What makes this winery appealing is the combination of hand-made wines with Mediterranean-influenced country-style food served in their tiny and intimate eatery reminiscent of small Italian family-run restaurants. The menu is designed for 'grazing' — small tapas-like plates of flavoursome food focusing on fresh local produce including fresh bread baked daily. In addition to wine, Cassito Miro also grows olives and produces its own oil and pickled olives. Stripped of any pretension, Cassito Miro will appeal to those who appreciate hand-crafted wines combined with food made with passion.

Bordeaux blends/Bordeaux style

Traditionally a Bordeaux blend is a mixture of six varieties in varying percentages which all add different qualities to the finished wine:

Cabernet Sauvignon	*body and tannin*
Merlot	*softness, roundness*
Cabernet Franc	*colour, aroma and freshness*
Petit Verdot	*perfume, colour, tannin and structure*
Malbec	*deep colour and tannin*
Carmenère	*colour and tannin*

And in the beginning there was Goldwater. The first vineyard to be established on Waiheke Island, in 1978, Goldwater produced its first vintage in 1982; and while the focus is still on red, Goldwater now also grows Chardonnay on Waiheke. Additional grapes are brought in from Marlborough (Sauvignon Blanc and Chardonnay), and from the famous Gimblett Gravels in Hawke's Bay (Merlot). The tasting room is in the original winery, and unusually for Waiheke Goldwater does not charge for tasting. On the last Friday of every month Goldwater holds a Long Lunch for which bookings are essential.

Gimblett Gravels

Established in 2001, Gimblett Gravels represents a group of New Zealand wineries and winemakers with land in this premium wine-growing area of Hawke's Bay. The Gimblett Gravels Appellation covers 800 hectares and is strictly determined by the gravelly soils laid by the Ngaruroro River after a great flood in the 1860s. The soil structure has a thin topsoil over free-draining gravels and is especially suited to growing red grape varieties.

Goldwater Estate

18 Causeway Road Putiki Bay

Labels **Goldwater**

Specialisation **Bordeaux-style blends**
Merlot
Chardonnay

Opening hours
Dec–Feb
   Daily 12 noon–4 pm
Mar–Nov
   Wed–Fri 12 noon–2 pm
   Sat/Sun 12 noon–4 pm
Lunch
   27 Dec–7 Jan
      Daily 11 am–4 pm
   13 Jan–6 Feb
      Sat/Sun 11 am–4 pm

Tasting   **No charge**
Phone   **09 372 7493**
Website
www.goldwaterwine.com

Kennedy Point Vineyard

**44 Donald Bruce Road
Kennedy Point**

Labels **Kennedy Point**

Specialisation **Syrah
Cabernet Sauvignon**

Opening hours
**Sat 2 pm–4 pm all year round
Labour Weekend
 Sat/Sun/Mon 12 noon–4 pm
26 Dec–14 Jan daily 12 noon–4 pm
Jan–Apr Sat/Sun 12 noon–4 pm
Lunch same times as above**

Tasting **$5 for three wines**
Phone **09 372 5600**
Website
www.kennedypointvineyard.com

Set amongst ancient pohutukawa trees, Kennedy Point is a small three-hectare vineyard producing wine from grapes grown on Waiheke Island, with the exception of Sauvignon Blanc which is sourced from growers in Marlborough. Bordeaux-style blends are its strength, along with its Syrah, which is unusually blended with a small percentage of Viognier. The small tasting room is located high above Te Putiki Bay, and from the deck the water is glimpsed through huge pohutukawa which are spectacular when in flower in December. In addition to wine, Kennedy Point grows olives and produces its own oil (which is also available for tasting), as well as a pohutukawa/manuka-blend honey from hives set amongst the trees. Kennedy Point offers a vineyard tour on the weekend at 3 pm with a focus on what is happening around the winery at that particular time, and also has accommodation available.

The winery offers a simple menu of tasting platters and wine is available by both the glass and the bottle. Kennedy Point does not serve coffee – why come to a winery to drink coffee?

Mudbrick has become an iconic Waiheke Island institution, and with very good reason. The vineyard was established in 1992 by Nick and Robyn Jones (who still own and run Mudbrick today), producing their first vintage in 1996 and at the same time opening a restaurant which established a reputation for excellent food matched with wine — a reputation Mudbrick has continued to maintain. In the style of European wineries, Mudbrick has grown in an attractive, organic way with buildings being added here and there, with an outcome that is both stylish and relaxed. The location is magnificent with land, sea and sky views over the Hauraki Gulf and Auckland city, making this an appealing spot both during the day and by night. The views are even more spectacular from the trig viewpoint behind the winery.

Two vineyards, one surrounding Mudbrick at Oneroa and the other at Onetangi, produce a broad range of wines from the awarding-winning Bordeaux-style reds to whites such as Chardonnay and Riesling, all processed using time-honoured winemaking techniques.

The fine dining restaurant is in a class of its own, with an emphasis on fresh local produce and excellent wines, and complemented by the organic potager gardens that surround the winery.

Mudbrick Vineyard

Church Bay Road
Oneroa

Labels **Mudbrick**

Specialisation **Syrah**
Bordeaux-style blends
Chardonnay

Opening hours
Daily 10.30 am–5 pm
Lunch 11.30 am–3 pm
Dinner from 6 pm

Tasting **$5 for eight wines**
Phone **09 372 9050**
Website **www.mudbrick.co.nz**

Obsidian Vineyard

Te Makiri Road
Onetangi

Labels **Obsidian**
        Weeping Sands

Specialisation **Bordeaux-style blends**
                Syrah
                Viognier

Opening hours
Jan–Mar daily 11 am–4 pm
Rest of year by appointment

Tasting **Casual visitors no charge,
         groups small charge**

Phone **09 372 6100**

Website **www.obsidian.co.nz**

Tucked away in a sunny valley behind Onetangi Beach, Obsidian is a small vineyard growing nine different varieties of grape on its nine hectares. Along with five Bordeaux varieties Obsidian also grows Syrah, Pinot Gris and Viognier, with Montepulciano due to come on-stream in 2007.

The location of Obsidian in a sheltered valley means regular summer temperatures above 30 degrees, ideal for ripening red grapes, and also making for a very pleasant spot to enjoy winter sunshine. The rustic terrace alongside the raupo and the native plantings makes for a very attractive picnic and wine-tasting experience.

Tucked away in the eastern end of the island this charming vineyard is well worth making the effort to get there. Set amongst the vines with a glimpse of the sea beyond, this rustic winery and café have a distinct Pacific flavour and a relaxed atmosphere. Moreover, Passage Rock is no slouch when it comes to producing wine. Its Syrah has consistently won awards, and it produces some very fine Bordeaux-style blends. All the wines produced are from the vineyard around this family-owned winery, with the exception of the Chardonnay which comes from Canterbury. Also very popular is the additive-free grape juice 'The Naked Grape' made from Merlot grapes.

The restaurant area is open for lunch with an emphasis on simple, flavoursome food, and in particular they have a reputation for spectacularly tasty pizza. Wine is available with food by both the bottle and the glass.

Passage Rock Wines

438 Orapiu Road
Te Makutu Bay

Labels **Passage Rock**

Specialisation **Syrah**

Opening hours
12 noon–4 pm
  Aug–24 Dec Sat/Sun only
  27 Dec–31 Jan daily
  Feb/Mar Wed–Sun
  Apr Sat/Sun
  Closed May–July

Tasting **$5 for four wines**
Phone **09 372 7257**
Website
www.passagerockwines.co.nz

Peninsula Estate

52a Korora Road
Oneroa

Labels **Peninsula**

Specialisation **Bordeaux-style wines**
Chardonnay

Opening hours
Nov–Easter daily 11 am–2.30 pm

Tasting **$8 for three wines**

Phone **09 372 7866**

Website
www.peninsulaestate.com

This small, two-hectare vineyard is one of the older establishments on the island, and retains an intimate feel with its small café and winery in a simple barn-style building. Producing wines only from grapes grown on Waiheke, Peninsula is known for its Bordeaux-blend reds and its oaked Chardonnay. Peninsula offers tastings in a small barrel-lined corner of the actual winery, and now provides a simple lunch through the summer — the barbecued crayfish tails alone are worth the trip to this winery.

While you are there, make time to take the short walk up to the lookout on the hill above the winery which has superb views over Oneroa Beach and far out into the Hauraki Gulf, to Coromandel and Little and Great Barrier Islands.

One of the best-known and most popular Waiheke vineyards, Stonyridge is a Tuscan-style winery with a broad, north-facing terrace overlooking vines and olive trees, and with a view towards the rocky hills that give Stonyridge its name. The famous restaurant specialises in exciting New Zealand dishes with a focus on fresh produce sourced locally where possible, and organic if available. Food is served alfresco on the terrace with its stone floors and wooden decks, or in winter by the open fire. Or visitors can just relax with a glass or two of wine on the terraces taking in the sun or lounging in shade.

Not forgetting the wine: Stonyridge is recognised for its outstanding ultra-premium red wines including Larose, a Bordeaux-style red wine. The wines are organic, with no herbicides or pesticides having been used on the Waiheke vineyards for over 20 years. Wine grown from Waiheke grapes is bottled under the Stonyridge label, while grapes grown off the island go under the Fallen Angel label.

In addition to wine and food, Stonyridge has the oldest established commercial olive grove in New Zealand, producing fine olive oil which is available for tasting and sale.

Check out the winery's website for details of its lively parties and events.

Stonyridge Vineyard

80 Onetangi Road Onetangi

Labels   **Stonyridge**
         Airfield
         Fallen Angel

Specialisation   **Bordeaux-style blends**

Opening hours
Daily 11.30 am–5 pm
Restaurant daily 11.30 am–3 pm
Winery tours 11.30 am Sat

Tasting   **$12 for four tastes**
        (can vary)

Phone   **09 372 8822**

Website   **www.stonyridge.com**

Te Whau

218 Te Whau Drive
Oneroa

Labels **Te Whau**

Specialisation **Bordeaux-style blends**
Chardonnay

Opening hours

Dec/Jan
   Daily 11 am–5 pm for tasting
   and lunch; dinner Thurs–Sat
Feb–Easter
   Daily except Tues, 11 am–5 pm
   for tasting and lunch; dinner Sat
Rest of year
   Fri–Sun 11 am–4.30 pm for
   tasting and lunch; dinner Sat

Tasting **$3 per tasting**
Phone **09 372 7191**
Website **www.tewhau.co.nz**

Te Whau must be one of the most spectacular sites of any vineyard in New Zealand. Located above Te Whau Bay, the winery and restaurant have views encompassing the inner gulf from Rangitoto and Tiritiri Matangi in the north, through downtown Auckland and south to the Firth of Thames, while far to the east lie the jagged peaks of the Coromandel ranges. Established in 1993, the strength of Te Whau is its Bordeaux blends and in particular its flagship wine The Point, which from its inception has consistently attracted accolades. Te Whau also produces tiny quantities of a superb Burgundian Chardonnay.

All wines are produced from grapes grown on the 2.5-hectare Waiheke property and processed in the winery located under the restaurant. Each vintage is hand-picked and hand-sorted, and bottles are individually capped and labelled and then stored in a climate-controlled barrel room dug deep into the hillside. This attention to detail has earned Te Whau numerous international and national accolades. Its wines are available only in limited quantities, through the vineyard and a few other selected outlets. Guided tours, conducted by the owner, are available for groups.

The restaurant is open and airy with floor-to-ceiling windows and wide folding doors taking every advantage of the fantastic views. The menu focuses on top-quality New Zealand ingredients, prepared simply with a definite European influence. The wine list is an attraction in itself, with over 600 of the very best New Zealand and international wines on offer.

The Ness valley just south of Clevedon is home to four small vineyards, and Inverness Estate is very typical of these. Yo and John Robinson moved to the valley in 1994 as a lifestyle change from a busy city life and now produce three wines, Cabernet Franc, Semillon and Chardonnay, which are made only from grapes grown on the property and carefully hand-picked. Their approach to wine is relaxed and friendly, and in addition to their enthusiasm for wine, they also breed Spanish horses and exhibit art by Sher Booth on their spacious property set in rambling gardens.

Inverness wines are available only from their vineyard and through selected restaurants.

Inverness Estate

Ness Valley Road
Clevedon

Labels **Inverness**

Specialisation **Cabernet Franc**
Chardonnay
Semillion

Opening hours
Sat/Sun 10 am–4 pm

Tasting **No charge**
Phone **09 292 8710**
Website **www.inverness.co.nz**

Phylloxera

In the second half of the nineteenth century, the vineyards of Europe were devastated by a little parasite insect called *Phylloxera*. *Phylloxera* gradually destroyed whole vineyards by eating and poisoning the roots and, due to the international trade of vine cuttings, eventually affected vineyards all over Europe, South Africa, Australia and New Zealand. The problem today has been overcome by the use of resistant or tolerant root-stock. This involves grafting a scion onto the roots of the resistant American native species, and does not interfere with the development of the wine grapes.

Villa Maria Estate

118 Montgomerie Road Mangere

Labels Villa Maria

Specialisation Pinot Noir
Sauvignon Blanc
Syrah
Merlot
Chardonnay
Pinot Gris
Viognier

Opening hours
Mon–Fri 9 am–6 pm
Sat/Sun 10 am–5 pm
Tours daily 11 am/3 pm

Tasting $5 for six tastings
Private Bin
$10 for six tastings
Cellar Selection
$15 for six tastings
Reserve

Phone 09 255 0666

Website www.villamaria.co.nz

It is easy to dismiss Villa Maria as another industrial vineyard producing supermarket wine, but think again. Family-owned, Villa Maria has won more awards than any other winery, with accolades totalling well over 2000 international and national awards. Guided by the overarching philosophy of owner and manager George Fistonich of making quality wines that he himself would like to drink, Villa Maria wines achieve a consistent quality that few other large or small wineries can match.

Villa Maria's architecturally award-winning complex is not only visually impressive, but is equally impressive as a working winery. From the state-of-the art bottling line to the more traditional barrel room, Villa Maria has combined the latest technology with age-old winemaking techniques to produce its huge range of wines. Sourcing quality grapes from both company-owned vineyards and contract growers around New Zealand, the winery employs techniques that include both mechanical and hand-harvesting, and small batch fermentation to ensure that the character of the grapes is preserved throughout.

The location of the winery in the industrial area near the airport is not a place that is usually associated with wine. However, Villa Maria was established in the area in 1961, and from a few acres around the winery it has now grown to one of New Zealand's flagship wineries. In addition to bottling all the wines produced by Villa Maria, the modern winery at Mangere has a stylish, open tasting area looking out over lawns, a pond and a small local vineyard. On offer are wine tasting, platter food and wine by the glass and bottle. The vineyard at Mangere is not just for show, but grows trophy-winning Chardonnay and Gewürztraminer.

Villa Maria also has excellent tours of the impressive winery each day at 11 am and 3 pm; this takes around half an hour (a charge applies).

As sponsors of the Auckland Philharmonic Orchestra, Villa Maria hosts the Mazda Summer Matinee, an outdoor concert in the vineyard held in the summer, as well as other concerts and events.

Vin Alto is a little slice of Italian heaven dropped into the hills high above Clevedon. One of the few New Zealand vineyards specialising in Italian-style wine, this winery produces a range of unusual varieties and blends, and all the grapes are hand-picked and processed to maintain quality. Situated on the slopes of the hills above Clevedon, the land was especially chosen for the Italian varieties as it has a climate that is drier and windier than the more sheltered and humid valley below. Not only will you find wines such as Arneis and Pinot Grigio, but Vin Alto also processes the grapes in a traditional manner to produce distinctively flavoured Italian-style wines. In addition to the 20 hectares of grapes, Vin Alto also grows olives and farms deer and there are even a couple of friendly donkeys.

However, Vin Alto is not just known for its Italian wines. Enzo and Margaret Bettio also run a traditional Italian enoteca at the weekends. Tracing its origins back to Roman times, an enoteca is an inn serving local wine with regional food, and at Vin Alto this tradition lives on. Beautiful small dishes of fresh seasonal food are served over the course of an afternoon, and each dish is matched with the appropriate wine. No need to order wine and fuss about a menu; just sit down and a parade of delicious food and tasty wines magically appears over the next four hours. In the traditional style Vin Alto does not have a chef, but family and friends cook for a limited number of guests. Hand-made cheese, freshly baked bread, home-made Italian pasta and excellent local produce are complemented by wines picked by Enzo to match the food. The meal finishes with delicious liqueurs such as limoncello, also made at Vin Alto. Reservations are essential.

In addition to excellent food and wine, the building has its own delights. The huge ceiling beams are from the old Devonport wharf, and the doors and much of the timber work are recycled wood. Take some time to view the cabinets around the walls. One holds an amazing collection of corkscrews, the oldest of which dates to 1790, while others hold collections of glass and decanters of which some date back hundreds of years.

Vin Alto

424 Creightons Road
Clevedon

Labels   Vin Alto
      Clevedon Hills
      Leighton

Specialisation   Italian-style wines –
      Celaio
      Pinot Grigio
      Ritorno
      Retico
      Cassis
      Limoncello

Opening hours
Mon–Fri 10 am–4 pm
Sat/Sun 11 am–4.30 pm
Enoteca
  Oct–Mar Sat/Sun
  Apr–Sep Sun only

Tasting   No charge
Phone   09 292 8845
Website   www.vinalto.com

Mills Reef

143 Moffat Road
Bethlehem, Tauranga

Labels Mills Reef

Specialisation Bordeaux-style blends
Syrah

Opening hours
Daily 10 am–5 pm
Lunch daily
Dinner by reservation

Tasting No charge

Phone 07 576 8800

Website www.millsreef.co.nz

Mills Reef also holds
an annual concert
in the vineyard,
but with numbers
limited to 5000 this
concert sells out
well in advance.

There is something immediately appealing about visiting a winery in Bethlehem and this smart, modern winery does not disappoint. Hugely popular with both locals and visitors, the spacious winery combines a tasting room and a fine dining restaurant with views out to the Kaimai Ranges. Although vineyards adjoin the winery, all of the grapes are sourced in from the Hawke's Bay (including the famous Gimblett Gravels), and processed at Tauranga. The range of wines is extensive across both whites and reds, and Mills Reef can lay claim to over 500 medals, 14 Champion Wine Trophies and New Zealand Winemaker of the Year 2003 and 2004.

The tasting room is meticulously laid out with the full range of Mills Reef wines and the friendly staff are more than helpful to both the novice and the wine expert alike. Large windows from the tasting room overlook the production area, including the labelling and bottling area, while below is a small barrel room with wine maturing in casks of French oak.

The fine dining restaurant is open for brunch, lunch and dinner, but is often booked out well in advance so you need to plan ahead, especially in summer. However, it is open for coffee on a casual basis all day. In addition to indoor dining, the broad north-facing terrace features a feasting table, a massive wooden slab 15 cm thick, designed to accommodate larger groups. Alongside the terrace is a pétanque area with enough courts to host a tournament.

Arriving at Morton Estate is like walking into a wine label. The Cape Dutch style of the main winery building with its distinctive curved gable will be easily recognisable to anyone familiar with the labels of Morton Estate wines. Independently owned Morton Estate was established in 1975, and as the area around the Katikati winery is too wet for growing good wine grapes, Morton now sources grapes from its vineyards in both Hawke's Bay and Marlborough. Famous for its Chardonnay, the vineyard offers wine tasting across a wide variety of styles, and next door is Morton's restaurant offering fine dining for both dinner and lunch in a pleasant, airy atmosphere opening on to a sheltered courtyard alongside the vineyard.

Morton Estate Wines

State Highway 2
Just south of Katikati

Labels Morton Estate
        Coniglio

Specialisation Chardonnay
                Methode Traditionelle

Opening hours
Daily 9.30 am–5 pm

Tasting No charge
Phone 07 552 0795
       restaurant 07 552 0620
Website
www.mortonestatewines.co.nz

Ohinemuri Estate

Moresby Street
Karangahake
(off State Highway 2 between Paeroa and Waihi)

Labels **Ohinemuri**

Specialisation **Gewürztraminer**
Riesling

Opening hours
Late Oct–late Apr
Daily 10 am–5 pm
Closed Christmas Day
Rest of year
Wed–Sun 10 am–5 pm

Tasting **$5, refunded with**
purchase

Phone **07 862 8874**

Website **www.ohinemuri.co.nz**

Established in 1989 and located in converted stables, this boutique winery is set in the bush above the Ohinemuri River in the historic Karangahake Gorge. As the area is too wet to grow grapes, the winery imports white grapes from Gisborne and red grapes from the Hawke's Bay for processing on the Ohinemuri site. The winery produces Chardonnay, Riesling and Merlot Malbec, but it is the Gewürztraminer that is German winemaker Horst Hillerich's pride and joy.

In addition to offering wine tasting, there is casual dining for breakfast and lunch in the cosy restaurant featuring huge, weathered beams of the old stables and in the sheltered stone-paved courtyard. Coffee and cake are served at any time. The other buildings surrounding the stables are uniquely designed in a Latvian style. On Sundays a classical guitarist entertains lunchtime diners, and there is limited accommodation in a converted hayloft above the stables.

Once a bustling gold-mining town of over 5000 people, very little now remains of Karangahake. There are two popular walks, both of which start in the parking area below the winery.

Rongopai combines the history of two different parts of the New Zealand wine story. Rongopai winery was originally established east of Te Kauwhata in 1932 as this area was recognised as a distinct Waikato microclimate and attracted a wide range of orchardists; it was well known for pit and stone fruit as well as grapes. While the fortunes of the winery fluctuated over the years, Rongopai was revived in the early 1980s and was part of the change in the wine industry at that time. In 1995 Rongopai purchased the former Viticulture Research Station and moved operations to this building.

The research station was founded in 1902, as part of a New Zealand government initiative to expand the wine industry, and was headed by Italian Romeo Bragato. It is said that Bragato established the research facility at Te Kauwhata partly because of its unique microclimate, but also because the area north of Huntly reminded him of his native Italy.

Now a Class A historic building, Rongopai is set among old established trees and in the grounds by the cellar is a huge restored oak wine barrel, acquired from Germany in 1921.

Over the years Rongopai has been less and less reliant on the unreliable Waikato vineyards, which often fail to produce sufficient grapes of quality to make the wines that Rongopai requires. Now almost the entire production is from vineyards all around the country, with only a small amount of Sauvignon Blanc being grown in Te Kauwhata. Of particular note is Rongopai's late harvest dessert wine Noble Late, which has won prestigious international awards as well as gold at the 2004 Royal Easter Show.

Rongopai Wines

55 Te Kauwhata Road
Te Kauwhata

Labels **Rongopai**
Ballochdale
Ultimo

Specialisation **Late harvest dessert wines**
Sauvignon Blanc
Merlot

Opening hours
Mon–Fri 9 am–5 pm

Tasting **No charge**
Phone **07 826 3981**
Website
www.rongopaiwines.co.nz

Wishart Estate Winery

Huka Falls Road
Taupo

Labels **Wishart Estate**

Specialisation **Sauvignon Blanc**
Syrah
Chardonnay

Opening hours
Labour Weekend–end Feb
  Daily 10 am–5 pm
Rest of year
  Wed–Sun 10 am–5 pm

Tasting **No charge**
Phone **07 378 5426**
Website
www.wishartwinery.co.nz

This winery is not quite what it seems. Owing to roading restrictions, Hawke's Bay winemakers Wishart Estate Winery cleverly decided to open a cellar in the tourist mecca of Taupo and at the same time experimented with growing grapes in Taupo.

The current owners of Wishart, brothers Don and Robbie Bird, are fourth-generation Hawke's Bay winemakers with connections to Glenvale Wines, now Esk Valley Wines. Their 13-hectare vineyard at Bay View, north of Napier, produces a wide range of wines including Sauvignon Blanc, Chardonnay, Merlot and Syrah as well as Muscat, dessert Merlot and a Merlot Rosé.

However, the cellar-door operation is not merely a sales outlet as Wishart planted one hectare of Pinot Noir in 2001, producing a respectable vintage in 2005 under the label Lonely Mountain Pinot Noir. This proved that good grapes can be grown in the Taupo area, but the soil is a challenge with a very thin layer of topsoil over a deep layer of volcanic pumice, and Wishart remains the only commercial vineyard in the Taupo area. A glass-sided case in the tasting room displays a good example of the free-draining soils of the Taupo vineyard. The tasting room is pleasant and spacious with views over the lake, and a special feature is that advice is given about matching food and wine.

Shiraz/Syrah/Hermitage

Depending on just where you are from, or the predilections of the winery or winemaker, Shiraz, Syrah and Hermitage are one and the same. It is said that the Syrah grape was originally brought to Western Europe from Shiraz in Iran by returning crusaders.

If the beach and wine are your ideal combination, then Amor-Bendall is your ideal winery. Situated across the road from the sands of world-famous Wainui Beach, this winery lays claim to the mostly easterly winery in the world and, of course, the first winery to see the sun each day. Its label reflects its location and is in fact a sea and sand adaptation of the view of Wainui Beach.

Unusually, Amor-Bendall does not own any vineyards but contracts out the grape-growing to Poverty Bay farmers and concentrates on making and marketing wine. The range is impressive, with a strong focus on white wine but offering a good range of red as well. Their Gewürztraminer and Chardonnays in particular have picked up an impressive array of awards.

So if the idea of a relaxed wine-tasting with sandy feet and salty hair appeals or you fancy a good bottle of wine with dinner, then drop in and see the folk at Amor-Bendall. Keep an eye out for their mobile crushing unit often parked at the back of the tasting room and designed to move from vineyard to vineyard during harvest time.

Amor-Bendall Wines

24 Moana Road
Wainui Beach

Labels **Amor-Bendall**

Specialisation **Chardonnay
Sauvignon**

Opening hours
Summer
    Daily 10 am–6 pm
Winter
    Mon–Fri 10 am–6pm
    Sat/Sun 1 pm–6 pm

Tasting **No charge**
Phone **06 868 0928**
Website **www.amor.bendall.co.nz**

Grappa

Grappa is an aromatic Italian grape brandy distilled from pomace, the grape residue including skins, seeds and stalks left after pressing and juice extraction. Distilled to give between 40% and 60% alcohol, grappa is an acquired taste; flavours are dependent on the quality and the grape variety used. The best grappas can be off-dry and floral, but most are harsh, fiery and youthful. Eau de vie de marc is the French equivalent, with excellent products from Burgundy and Champagne in particular.

Bushmere Estate

166 Main Road
Makaraka

Labels **Bushmere**

Specialisation **Chardonnay**
Gewürztraminer

Opening hours
Dec–Feb
Thurs–Sun 11 am–5 pm
Mar–Nov
Fri–Sun 11 am–5 pm

Tasting **$5, refundable with**
purchase

Phone **06 868 9393**

Website **www.bushmere.com**

Located on the main road south, this long-established family-owned vineyard relaunched their wines under the new Bushmere label in 2005 and turned an old kiwifruit pack house into the most stylish winery restaurant in Poverty Bay.

The pack house is now totally unrecognisable, transformed into a modern café that has been pulling in the local crowd with fresh, light summer food combined with popular events. Open and airy, the café opens out on to a lawn alongside the vines, and the delicate inlaid paua chips on the concrete floor and local art on the walls add a distinct New Zealand touch. During summer Bushmere provides live music on a Sunday afternoon, and on Boxing Day night Opera in the Vines is very popular, although bookings are essential as it is limited to 200 people. So if you are looking to taste wine, have a coffee and good food or just a relaxing glass of wine, Bushmere is just the spot when you are visiting Gisborne.

In addition to its award-winning Chardonnay and Gewürztraminer, Bushmere also produces Merlot and Rose.

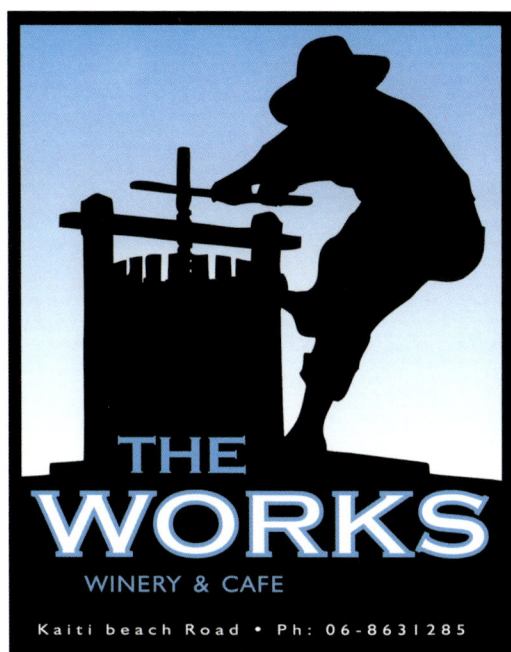

Goldenvines Estate/The Works Cafe

Kaiti Beach Road
Gisborne

Labels **Goldenvines**

Specialisation **Oaked Chardonnay**
Gewürztraminer
Merlot
Sauvignon Blanc

Opening hours
Daily from 10 am

Tasting **$10 for seven tastings**
and a cheese board

Phone **06 863 1285**

Website **www.goldenvines.co.nz**

The name Goldenvines is derived from the vineyards in the area known as The Golden Slope, northwest of Gisborne, and noted for producing grapes that turn into gold-award-winning Chardonnay wines. The winery called The Gisborne Wine Company is situated in the city at the foot of Kaiti Hill in an historic brick freezing works built in 1904. The brick and concrete building with its large cool spaces is ideal for wine production and storage, and makes a very smart restaurant space. Goldenvines is made by winemaker John Thorpe, with other labels including John's own label, Longbush.

The Works Cafe in the same building is an attractive spacious restaurant with a wide sunny terrace catching the afternoon sun, and overlooking the river and port. It offers alfresco lunch and fine dining in the evening. The Works wine list features a range of Gisborne wines, and the menu matches wines with the food. Wine tasting, accompanied by wine-tasting notes and a cheese board, is available 10–11 am and 4–5 pm in a relaxed manner on large comfy couches.

Kirkpatrick Estate Winery — KEW

569 Wharekopae Road
Patutahi Plateau
Gisborne

Labels KEW

Specialisation Wild Rose
Merlot
Chardonnay
Gewürztraminer

Opening hours
Summer
Daily 11 am–5 pm
Autumn and spring
Fri–Mon 11 am–4 pm
Winter
Sat and Sun 12 noon–4 pm

Tasting $10 for 14 wines
Phone 06 862 7722
Website www.kew.co.nz

The KEW label was established in 2004 by Simon Kirkpatrick, though the vineyard, Gisborne's only terraced one, was planted long before that. Within a short period, KEW has won an impressive array of awards across its range of wines that include Chardonnay, Merlot, Rose and Malbec. All wines are produced from this one vineyard, and KEW uses only single varietals for its wines. The small terraced hill above the winery is carefully planted with varieties that benefit from the steep site, and another area was specially contoured to grow Merlot. It was from this planting that KEW's 2005 Top Flat Reserve Merlot originated, and which won the 2006 Best of the Best Award for that year. The Kirkpatricks have farmed in this area for 150 years.

The attractive winery offers wine tasting and antipasto platters, or you can bring a picnic and enjoy the garden in front of the winery building with a glass or two of wine. Local olive oils are also available. A lookout at the top of the hill has great views over Poverty Bay and the surrounding hills.

Very popular with locals and visitors alike, The Millton Vineyard is well known for its award-winning certified organic wines and recognised as a pioneer in this field. Now covering 30 hectares in four separate vineyards in the Manutuke region, The Millton Vineyard was established as a bio-dynamic organic vineyard in 1984 along Te Arai River. This means that no insecticide, herbicide, systemic fungicide or soluble fertilisers are used in the vineyard. Grapes have been grown on this property since the 1960s.

Like most Poverty Bay vineyards, The Millton Vineyard is strong on white wine, though it also produces Merlot, Pinot Noir, Malbec and Syrah. All the wines are from single vineyards and these are identified on the label (for example Te Arai Chenin Blanc, Opou Vineyard Chardonnay). The Millton Vineyard's premium wines are produced under the Clos De St Anne label, which comes from Naboth's Vineyard, a northeastern-facing hill slope in the foothills of Poverty Bay. It also produces two dessert wines from Viognier and Chardonnay grapes.

The tasting area is located in the large cool barrel room, and the lovely gardens with clipped hedges, old olive trees and large shade trees are a great spot for a picnic.

The Millton Vineyard

119 Papatu Road
Manutuke
Gisborne

Labels   The Millton Vineyard
        Clos De St Anne

Specialisation   Chenin Blanc
               Riesling

Opening hours
Labour Weekend–end Dec
   Mon–Sat 10 am–5 pm
Jan and Feb
   Daily 10 am–5 pm
Mar–Labour Weekend
   Mon–Fri 10 am–5pm

Tasting   Casual visitors no charge,
         groups call ahead

Phone   **06 862 8680**

Website   **www.millton.co.nz**

Esk Valley Estate

Main Road, Bay View Napier

Labels **Esk Valley**

Specialisation **Bordeaux-style blends**
Syrah
Sauvignon Blanc
Pinot Gris
Chenin Blanc
Riesling
Chardonnay
Verdelho

Opening hours
Daily 10 am–5 pm

Tasting **Casual visitors no charge**
Phone **06 872 7430**
Website **www.eskvalley.co.nz**

Established in 1933 by Robert Bird to produce fortified wines, Esk Valley's winery is a series of rambling historical buildings that retain a distinct 1940s charm. Further contributing to the Italianate feel, a palm-lined drive and terraced gardens sit below the vineyard that is located on steep hillsides above the winery buildings. The Malbec, Merlot and Cabernet Franc grapes from this unique terrace location go into the winery's iconic wine, appropriately called The Terraces.

Now part of the Villa Maria group, Esk Valley under winemaker Gordon Russell retains a very strong sense of individuality, with all its wines made on site at Bay View using traditional winemaking techniques. Esk Valley produces a wide range of wines including Chardonnay, Pinot Gris, Merlot, Syrah, Rosé and Chenin Blanc, and is the only vineyard in New Zealand to bottle Verdelho. With an emphasis on handcrafting, several of the varieties are made only in very small quantities with limited distribution.

As well as wine tasting and sales, tours are available by appointment and the winery also hosts regular art exhibitions in a large, spacious room overlooking the sea.

One of New Zealand's oldest and best-known wineries, the Mission winery is located on a bluff above Taradale with extensive views over the Hawke's Bay plain, Napier city and the bay itself.

Originally established in 1851 by French Marist missionaries at Pakowhai (between Napier and Hastings), the mission moved to Meeanee in 1858. Grapes were planted to provide altar wine but by the 1870s the mission was providing red wine for sale. However, periodic flooding forced the mission to move to higher ground, and in 1909 the large wooden mission house was moved to the Taradale land which had been purchased for grape-growing in 1897. The small gothic chapel was added in 1914, but the entire mission suffered severe damage in the 1931 earthquake with two priests and seven students killed when the stone chapel collapsed.

Now no longer a seminary, Mission Estate has undergone extensive renovations in the last decade and today is a superb historical building on an equally superb site. In tandem, Mission has also significantly improved its wine quality and range, and now ranks alongside the best that Hawke's Bay has to offer. Producing a wide range of red and white wines, Mission excels in Chardonnay and red blends but also offers Rosé, Viognier, Merlot, ice wine, Gewürztraminer, Pinot Gris and Sauvignon Blanc.

Located in the old seminary building, the restaurant offers fine dining for both lunch and dinner with indoor and terrace options depending on the weather and with great views over the surrounding countryside. The tasting area is lined with historical photographs, and in addition to sampling wines and wine sales there are tours of the building and cellar available. A gallery specialises in local craft and art, ranging from jewellery and pottery through to paintings and furniture. However, Mission may be in danger of becoming a victim of its own success with some staff in dire need of a customer-service course.

Mission Estate Winery

**198 Church Road
Taradale, Napier**

Labels **Mission**

Specialisation **Chardonnay
Syrah
Cabernet Merlot
Cabernet Sauvignon**

Opening hours
**Mon–Sat
  9 am–5 pm
Sun
  10 am–4.30 pm
  (extended in summer)
Tours daily at 10.30 am and 2 pm**

Tasting **No charge**
Phone **06 845 9350**
Website **www.missionestate.co.nz**

Sacred Hill

**1003 Dartmoor Road
Puketapu, Napier**

Labels Sacred Hill

Specialisation Chardonnay
Bordeaux-style blends

Opening hours
Daily 11 am–5 pm Dec–Feb only
Closed Christmas, Boxing and
New Year's Days

Tasting Casual visitors no charge
Phone **06 844 0138**
Website **www.sacredhill.com**

Situated in the Dartmoor Valley alongside the Tutaekuri River, west of Napier, Sacred Hill is located on part of a sheep and beef farm owned by brothers Dave and Mark Mason, who in the mid-'80s decided to diversify into grapes. In the intervening 20 years Sacred Hill has gone from strength to strength, and now the two vineyards in the river valley provide Chardonnay, Sauvignon Blanc, Merlot and Cabernet Sauvignon; a further vineyard on the Gimblett Gravels grows the Bordeaux varietals; and from Marlborough come Sauvignon Blanc and Pinot Noir grapes.

The old winery and barrel room are now a very attractive cellar-door facility and one of Hawke's Bay's most popular destinations, despite being more distant than other wineries. Overhung with lush vines and built with timber from old bridge and wharf piles, Sacred Hill is set amongst grand old trees and green lawns, and is the ideal spot to picnic, play pétanque and croquet, or enjoy a glass or more of good wine in relaxed surroundings.

Oak ageing/wine barrels

Ageing in oak imparts toasty, smoky vanilla and butter flavours to wine; barrels are sourced from France, Germany, the USA and Hungary. Winemakers can choose not only wood from different forests in France (e.g. Nevers, Tioneais, Limousin) to influence how their wine ages, but also barrels that have been charred to produced a light, medium or heavy toast that will also flavour the wine.

Wine barrels generally last three to five years, after which time they impart virtually no flavour to the wine. 'Oaky flavour' refers to the toasty, smoky vanilla smell and flavour that comes from ageing the wine in oak barrels after fermentation.

The name Alpha Domus was created from an acronym of the first letters of the family's Christian names, which make up the word 'alpha' (the first letter of the Greek alphabet), plus 'domus' which is Latin for 'house'. The distinct Alpha Domus label, with its colourful Tiger Moth, is a reflection of the winery's close proximity to Bridge Pa airfield; the aviation theme is carried through into the names of its wines (e.g. The Aviator).

Producing only single-estate wines, Alpha Domus has 35 hectares in grapes in two vineyards within just three kilometres of each other; and has not only established a reputation for Bordeaux-style reds, but has also won awards for its Sauvignon Blanc, Viognier and dessert wines.

Wine tasting is a simple affair with the tasting area located in the winery itself, surrounded by tanks of fermenting grape juice, while outside a pleasant shaded area is just the spot for a relaxing picnic or glass of wine.

More adventurous visitors can take a ride in a vintage aeroplane over the vineyards in the area, from the Bridge Pa aerodrome, on Harvest Hawke's Bay weekend.

Alpha Domus

1829 Maraekakaho Road
Bridge Pa, Hastings

Labels Alpha Domus

Specialisation Bordeaux-style
varietal reds
Chardonnay
Viognier
Dessert wines

Opening hours
Labour Weekend–Easter
  Daily 10 am–5 pm
Rest of year
  Fri–Mon 10 am–4 pm

Tasting Casual visitors no charge

Phone 06 879 6752

Website www.alphadomus.co.nz

C J Pask Winery

1133 Omahu Road
Hastings

Labels **C J Pask**

Specialisation **Cabernet Merlot**
Malbec
Syrah
Merlot
Chardonnay

Opening hours
Mon–Sat 9 am–5 pm
Sun 10 am–4 pm

Tasting **Casual visitors no charge**

Phone **06 879 7906**

Website **www.cjpask.co.nz**

Founded by Chris Pask in 1981, these vineyards cover 100 hectares of the Gimblett Gravels on the very outskirts of Hastings, and now produce over 50,000 cases of wine annually. C J Pask offers three ranges: Declaration, Gimblett Road and Roy's Hill — the Declaration wines are produced only in exceptional vintages and even then only in modest quantities, and this range has won numerous awards for C J Pask over the years for both its Chardonnay and its reds.

The tasting room in Omahu Road is a friendly place, located in the cool atmosphere of the barrel room with oak casks towering in stacks the length of the winery. The walls are lined with colourful and stylish posters advertising the annual Hawke's Bay Charity Auction, and as a company they have also taken considerable care to work in an environmentally sustainable fashion.

Classic varieties

The original and classic varieties of grape are as follows:

Red	White
Pinot Noir	Sauvignon Blanc
Cabernet Sauvignon	Riesling
Merlot	Chardonnay
Syrah/Shiraz	Chenin Blanc

This smart little vineyard of just 16 hectares is just the place if you are interested in tasting wines grown on Hawke's Bay's famous Gimblett Gravels. Producing just 5000 cases annually, Hatton Estate grows all its wines on this single family-owned vineyard, and in addition to Cabernet-Sauvignon-based reds, Hatton Estate also produces excellent Syrah, Chardonnay and Merlot blends. Its 2004 Tahi — Cabernet Sauvignon/Merlot/Cabernet Franc — won a gold and a trophy at the 2006 Air New Zealand Wine Awards, and it is the Hatton 1998 vintage that is featured on the wine list at Gordon Ramsay's Michelin three-star London restaurant.

Keen to improve the visitor's wine knowledge, Hatton Estate's simple tasting room is a casual and friendly affair, tucked into a corner of the winery's barrel room. The staff taste with visitors so that the information imparted is accurate and relates to the actual wine being tasted. The staff at Hatton are also happy to show visitors aspects of the winery operation that are occurring at the time.

Hatton Estate

124 Gimblett Road Hastings

Labels **Hatton Estate**

Specialisation **Cabernet Sauvignon reds**

Opening hours
Summer
 Daily 10 am–4.30 pm
Winter
 Mon–Sat 10 am–4 pm

Tasting   **Casual visitors no charge**

Phone   **06 870 4777**

Website **www.hattonestate.com**

Tannin

Predominately a feature of red wines, tannin is drawn from the grape skins, pips and stems and is dissolved in the juice during fermentation. It is an essential constituent of wine, giving character and long-lasting qualities. Strong tannins give the wine that furry feeling on our teeth, in a similar way to a strong cup of tea or an unripe banana.

Kemblefield Estate Winery

Kemblefield Terrace
Mangatahi

Labels **Kemblefield**

Specialisation **Zinfandel**

Opening hours
Mon–Fri 9 am–5 pm
Sat/Sun 10.30 am–4.30 pm

Tasting **Casual visitors no charge**

Phone **06 874 9649**

Website **www.kemblefield.co.nz**

It is surprising that Zinfandel, a very popular Californian red wine, is produced by only two wineries in New Zealand. What is not surprising is that Kemblefield is one of these wineries, as John Kemble is a Californian native with considerable US qualifications and experience. John began planting in 1992 on the well-drained terraces located alongside the Ngaruroro River at Mangatahi, leading a trend that has seen the area expand as a prime grape-growing location over the past 15 years. The winery at Kemblefield is spacious and open, sitting high above the river with magnificent views over the river valley and beyond. Modern and stylish, the winery building features extensive use of river stone, from the arched courtyard with its fountain through to the spacious interior and the broad north-facing terrace.

John Kemble is particular in sourcing his grape varieties and grows most of his own root stock, including Zinfandel from cuttings imported in 1994 from California's Ravenswood Winery. In addition Kemblefield grows Chardonnay, Gewürztraminer, Sauvignon Blanc, Merlot, Malbec, Pinot Gris, Cabernet Sauvignon and Cabernet Franc, and all the wine comes from this one 90-hectare vineyard.

In addition to wine tasting and sales, a picnic food selection is available.

Brix (°Bx)

This is a measurement of the ratio of dissolved sucrose/sugar to water in a liquid. For example, 25°Bx means there are 25 grams of sucrose/sugar and 75 grams of water in 100 grams of the solution. The higher the brix reading, the riper the grapes, and this figure is monitored along with pH (acidity) to determine the best time to harvest.

Newly established in 2000, Lime Rock harvested their first grapes from their single vineyard in 2004. The vineyard is a few kilometres west of Waipawa, central Hawke's Bay, and just 35 minutes south of Hastings. Sitting at 230 to 270 metres above sea level and further inland than the other Hawke's Bay wineries, the climate here is much cooler than near the coast and in recent years has been identified as being climatically similar to Marlborough — and therefore ideal for growing Sauvignon Blanc. The slope of the hill alleviates the frost, and the winery's name is perfect, reflecting the soil profile that consists of a thin layer of topsoil over a hill of limestone. A small limestone outcrop by the winery is a good illustration of just how thin the topsoil really is.

The crumbling limestone is full of fossilised sea life such as oysters, scallops and barnacles from an age when this land was under the sea, and some of these fossils are on display in the tasting room. While you are there take a short walk up through the vines to the top of the hill for spectacular views over the Waipawa River, across the central plain and to the Ruahine and Ruataniwha ranges.

Originally the family beef and sheep farm, Lime Rock also produces Pinot Noir, Pinot Gris, Merlot and small volumes of Riesling in addition to the Sauvignon Blanc. All the vines are hand-pruned and grapes are hand-picked. As well as tasting Lime Rock wines in the modest but friendly winery, visitors can taste extra virgin olive oil and saffron products by Ellsgrove, one of Hawke's Bays leading olive growers. Lime Rock also sells wine produced by the tiny winery Tukipo River Estate.

Lime Rock Wines

601 Tikokino Road Waipawa

Labels Lime Rock

Specialisation Pinot Noir
Sauvignon Blanc

Opening hours
Labour Weekend–end Feb
Sat/Sun 11 am–4 pm; other
times by arrangement — phone
Rosie Butler or Rodger Tynan

Tasting Casual visitors no charge

Phone 06 857 8247

Website www.limerock.co.nz

Matariki Wines

52 Kirkwood Road
Hastings

Labels **Matariki**

Specialisation **Gimblett Gravels reds**

Opening hours
Daily 9 am–5 pm

Tasting **Casual visitors no charge,
large groups by
appointment**

Phone **06 879 6226**

Website **www.matarikiwines.co.nz**

A privately owned family winery, Matariki takes its name from the constellation that appears around the shortest day and heralds the southern hemisphere New Year, known to Maori as Matariki. With the main vineyard on the Gimblett Gravels, and a further smaller site in the Tukituki valley near Te Mata, Matariki is strong in Bordeaux-type reds, but also produces Sangiovese, Rosé, Chardonnay and Sauvignon Blanc. In addition Matariki also produces its own balsamic vinegar and olive oils.

On the walls of the tasting room, Matariki has enlarged photos of the soil profiles of the Gimblett Gravels, clearly demonstrating why this area is so good for growing grapes. A layer of topsoil varying in depth overlays the gravels of the old Ngaruroro River bed, providing a fertile base for the grapes' roots but at the same time allowing excellent drainage.

Ngatarawa has a unique story in New Zealand wine-making history, intertwining Hawke's Bay racing history with long-established West Auckland winemakers the Corban family. Immigrating from Lebanon to New Zealand in 1891, Assid Corban planted his first vines in the Henderson Valley in 1902, thereby establishing a tradition of winemaking in the Corban family which flourishes to this day. In 1981 Harry Glazebrook and Alwyn Corban first planted vines at Ngatarawa on the gravelly soils of the old Ngaruroro River bed when very few others were growing grapes in the area. After 18 years of expansion the vineyard was sold to cousins Alwyn and Brian Corban, and today Ngatarawa is a medium-sized family-owned winery.

Sourcing grapes from a number of vineyards around the country as well as from Hawke's Bay, Ngatarawa produces a wide selection of wines in four ranges, from its very best reserve vintages under the Alwyn name through to everyday drinking wines, the Stables. Included are Chardonnay, Noble Harvest Riesling, Merlot-based reds, Sauvignon Blanc, Pinot Noir, Pinot Gris and Syrah.

The stables themselves were built in 1892, with very little altered in the intervening years, and are now smartly painted in white and green. Surrounded by rows of vines, the stables are in the heart of spacious lawns and gardens, complete with shade trees and a lily pond, an ideal spot for a picnic for all the family, children included. There is plenty of parking, including room for motor homes and excellent disabled access.

At Ngatarawa visitors have the opportunity to taste across a range of vintages as well as different varieties, and a number of wines are exclusive to the cellar door and not available elsewhere.

Ngatarawa Wines

305 Ngatarawa Road Bridge Pa, Hastings

Labels **Ngatarawa**
Glazebrook

Specialisation **Chardonnay**
Merlot-based reds
Dessert wines

Opening hours
Labour Weekend–Easter
  Daily 10 am–5 pm
Rest of year
  Daily 11 am–4 pm

Tasting **Casual visitors no charge,**
groups by appointment

Phone **06 879 7603**

Website **www.ngatarawa.co.nz**

Sileni Estates

2016 Maraekakaho Road Bridge Pa, Hastings

Labels **Sileni**

Specialisation **Merlot blends**
Chardonnay
Sauvignon Blanc
Syrah
Semillon

Opening hours
Daily 10 am–5 pm
Tours 11 am/2 pm
Lunch daily from 11 am
Dinner Thurs/Fri/Sat from 6 pm

Tasting **$2 for three wines,**
$5 for a full range,
refundable with purchase
(wine cellar or restaurant)

Phone **06 879 8768**

Website **www.sileni.co.nz**

Arriving at Sileni is grand. Situated down a long driveway through extensive rows of vines, the winery has a striking modern profile set low against tawny hills, so typical of Hawke's Bay. Designed by Auckland architects Dodd, Paterson, Bukoski and Rhem, the building sits naturally on the landscape, is eminently functional, and yet at the same time has a sophistication that is both international and New Zealand in style.

Established in 1999, the winery is named after the Sileni who appear in Roman mythology alongside Bacchus the Greek god of wine adopted by the Romans. Usually pictured as satyrs, the Sileni generally enjoyed life by celebrating good wine, good food and good company, and were said to have gifted King Midas his golden touch.

Sileni's wines cover a wide range from award-winning reds to export-quality whites, and include Merlot/Carbernet Franc/Malbec, Pinot Noir, Syrah, Semillon, Chardonnay, Sauvignon Blanc, Riesling, Pinot Gris, Rosé and dessert wines. But Sileni is more than a winery. The restaurant is now under the guidance of Head Chef Andy Glover, formerly of London's famous Cuckoo Club, a favourite haunt of Prince Harry; and Andy and his team also conduct the Sileni Estates Culinary School for those wanting to expand their cooking skills. The gourmet store is worth a trip in itself — on offer is an array of delicatessen food, sourced from the best of New Zealand and international fine foods, with special attention given to cheeses, chocolate, olive oils and balsamic vinegars.

While Sileni offers traditional wine tasting, it also has one-hour vineyard and winery tours plus tasting, and it is worthwhile checking out the website for Sileni's other food and wine experiences.

Arriving at Te Awa the first inclination is to sink quietly into a chair and never leave. Te Awa is the winery of everyone's dreams turned into reality. Relaxed and sophisticated, Te Awa is set deep amongst the vines and its rustic-barn style makes for an exceptionally pleasant lunch, whether under the trees, on the wide terrace, or in the cosy interior dining area. The food matches the ambience: Te Awa was runner-up in the Cuisine Restaurant of the Year Award 2006, combining the best of fresh New Zealand produce with contemporary cooking styles. It is a popular restaurant, and bookings are recommended.

Set on the Gimblett Gravels, the winery takes its name from the Maori Te Awa o Te Atua or River of God, referring to underground streams that run far beneath the gravelly soil, ideal for growing grapes. All Te Awa wines are single-estate and cover a wide range including Chardonnay, Sauvignon Blanc, Merlot, Pinotage Syrah and Te Awa's flagship red blend Boundary.

Te Awa Winery

2375 State Highway 50 Hastings

Labels **Te Awa**
Longlands

Specialisation **Chardonnay**
Sauvignon Blanc
Merlot-based reds

Opening hours
Daily 9 am–5 pm
Restaurant 12 noon–3 pm

Tasting **$5 for six wines,**
refunded on purchase

Phone **06 879 7602**

Website **www.teawa.com**

Triangle Red

**217 Ngatarawa Road
Bridge Pa, Hastings**

Labels Three individual vineyards:
Unison
Bushhawk
Bridge Pa

Specialisation Gimblett Gravel Reds

Opening hours
26 Dec–end Feb
Daily 11 am–4 pm
20 Oct–24 Dec
1 Mar–Queen's Birthday (early
June)
Fri/Sat/Sun 11 am–4 pm

Tasting Casual visitors no charge,
charges for special tasting
flights

Phone **0800 494 637**

Opened in October of 2006, Triangle Red is Hawke's Bay's only co-operative winery and is the outlet for three individual vineyards: Unison, Bushhawk and Bridge Pa. While Unison has its own cellar door, this is the only sales outlet for Bushhawk and Bridge Pa. The tasting room and café are set among the Pinot Gris vines of Bushhawk, and Bridge Pa's vineyard is just across the road. Bruce Helliwell, the owner of Unison, is the winemaker for the three vineyards, and all three have a strength in Bordeaux-style reds as well as Syrah and some whites.

The cellar-door facility is understated and con-temporary in style, and visitors will be led through the wine tasting by one of the owners of the three vineyards, an experience not always possible at larger vineyards. As well as wine tasting, Triangle Red offers platters and tasty pizzas from its outdoor pizza oven in the relaxed café alongside the tasting room. Also on offer is accommodation in two spacious apartments in the same building, with access to all facilities after the doors close to the public at 4 pm.

A visit to vineyards in Hawke's Bay would not be complete without a visit to Trinity Hill. With a greater variety of wines than any other New Zealand vineyard, Trinity Hill produces many of its wines in small boutique quantities rather than in bulk, and the range covers the classic varieties as well as the unusual Tempranillo and Montepulciano. While most of the wines come from grapes grown on the Gimblett Gravels at Trinity Hill, the winery also sources grapes from other Hawke's Bay vineyards, including Pinot Noir, Chardonnay and Sauvignon Blanc.

The striking modern winery has a distinct New Zealand style and is the work of well-known architect Richard Priest. At once both stylish and eminently suited to a working winery, the tasting room with its lofty high ceilings has views through large windows into the working winery and also displays contemporary New Zealand art. Great care has been taken with the gardens surrounding the winery which are popular for picnics, weddings and concerts, while behind the winery is a very pleasant sheltered courtyard, ideal to catch the sun on a winter's day. Picnic platters featuring local produce are available during summer.

Trinity Hill

2396 State Highway 50 Roy's Hill, Hastings

Labels Trinity Hill

Specialisation Chardonnay
Bordeaux-style reds
Syrah
Viognier
Tempranillo

Opening hours
Labour Weekend–Easter
Daily 10 am–5 pm
Rest of year
11 am–4 pm

Tasting Casual visitors no charge
Phone 06 879 7778
Website www.trinityhill.com

Unison Vineyard

2163 State Highway 50 Hastings

Labels **Unison**

Specialisation **Unison (a red blend) Syrah**

Opening hours
Mon–Sat 9 am–5 pm
Sun (summer only) 11 am–4 pm

Tasting **No charge**
Phone **06 879 7913**
Website
www.unisonvineyard.co.nz

One of the first vineyards to be established on the Gimblett Gravels, Unison is rapidly gaining a strong following for its superb reds. Unison's Syrah won the Air New Zealand Top Red Wine Award in 2005, and its own Merlot/Cabernet Sauvignon/Syrah blend, simply known as Unison, is sought after by red-wine drinkers in the know. Unison was the only New Zealand vineyard to be included in Jancis Robinson's list of '28 up-and-coming producers in the world'. The operation is small, only six hectares, but this allows winemaker Bruce Helliwell to personally ensure that the highest quality is strictly maintained through all the processes.

It also ensures friendly and personable service at the tasting room in the barrel-lined cellar tucked underground beneath the Helliwells' home. In addition to wine Unison also produces a traditional balsamic vinegar and olive oil, and offers accommodation in The Winemaker's Retreat.

Askerne Winery

267 Te Mata
Mangateretere Road
Havelock North

Labels **Askerne**

Specialisation **Dessert wines**
Chardonnay
Gewürztraminer

Opening hours
Mid-Dec–end Feb
  Daily 10 am–5 pm
Rest of year
  Sat/Sun/public holidays
  11 am–5 pm

Tasting **No charge**
Phone **06 877 2089**
Website **www.askerne.co.nz**

A small intimate winery, Askerne grows all its wines on the 20 hectares of vineyard just outside Havelock North. With a good reputation for producing fine white wines, including Chardonnay and Sauvignon Blanc, Askerne also produces Pinot Noir, Cabernet/Merlot and a Rosé. In more recent years it has been bottling some head-turning dessert wines, among them Noble Semillon, Botrytis Semillon and an excellent dessert Cabernet.

The wine tasting room is simple and friendly, set among the huge gum trees which feature on their label. The large shady trees are a great place for a picnic and there is a children's play area as well.

Black Barn Vineyards

Black Barn Road
Havelock North

Labels **Black Barn**

Specialisation **Chardonnay**
Sauvignon Blanc
Bordeaux-style blends

Opening hours
Daily 10 am–5 pm
Bistro Wed–Sun 12 noon–2.30 pm

Tasting **Casual visitors no charge,**
groups of five or more
$2 each

Phone **06 877 7985**

Website **www.blackbarn.com**

Simple and stylish, this winery has a retro-1950s feel with black weatherboards on a barn-like building which is at its heart modern and contemporary.

Covering just 10 hectares, Black Barn grows all its wines on the Havelock North property, and to ensure the best quality all the grapes are hand-picked and carefully processed. In addition the vineyard is further broken up into 28 sections which are processed individually for their differing qualities. While the focus is on Bordeaux-style reds, Black Barn also produces award-winning Chardonnay and Sauvignon Blanc.

The view from the bistro on the elevated lower slopes of the Te Mata hills is surprisingly expansive – the location does not give the impression of any great height, yet has a magnificent northerly outlook over the plain. The bistro, open only for lunch, has an emphasis on fresh Hawke's Bay produce and is very popular with locals. The small, sheltered courtyard with fig trees, leading to the bistro and tasting room, also has on one side a stand-alone art gallery specialising in works by important New Zealand artists.

Black Barn hosts a Growers' Market through the summer months as well as musical events in a purpose-built amphitheatre, and has luxury accommodation available at selected locations throughout the Hawke's Bay including at the vineyard.

One of the first vineyard restaurants to open in a rural area, Clearview is a clear favourite with both locals and visitors alike. With a relaxed atmosphere, Clearview is open and airy, catching the cool sea breezes in the summer; while in winter an open fire creates a cosy and cheery ambience. The emphasis is on fresh Hawke's Bay produce, including the liberal use of herbs from the large kitchen garden, and avocados and olive oil from their own olive groves. Clearview has won a Beef & Lamb Excellence Award every year since 1998. In addition to a long, lingering lunch, Clearview is also open for brunch, coffee or wine by the glass throughout the day, but bookings are essential for lunch, especially in summer.

The 13 hectares at Te Awanga produce high-quality wines, in particular the 20-year-old Chardonnay vines used to create Clearview's renowned Reserve Chardonnay. Still family-owned and -operated by Tim Turvey and Helma van den Berg, much of the restaurant design and landscaping was done by Tim and Helma, and over the years they have also planted avocado, bay and citrus trees, giving the vineyard a distinct Hawke's Bay feel with a Mediterranean touch. While this vineyard was established just 20 years ago (and uses very little insecticide), the property was once an early vineyard established by Anthony Vidal in 1915 and one 90-year-old olive tree still remains from this period.

The restaurant frequently hosts art exhibitions and accommodation is available in the Winemaker's Cottage.

Clearview Estate Winery and Restaurant

194 Clifton Road
Te Awanga

Labels **Clearview**

Specialisation **Chardonnay**

Opening hours
Labour Weekend–Easter
 10 am–5 pm daily
Rest of year
 Fri–Tues 10 am–5 pm

Tasting   No charge; bus groups
        and tours by appointment
        only
Phone   **06 875 0150**
Website
www.clearviewestate.co.nz

Craggy Range Giants Winery

253 Waimarama Road
Havelock North

Labels **Craggy Range**

Specialisation **Bordeaux-style blends**
Syrah
Merlot

Opening hours
Daily 10 am–5 pm
Restaurant
Labour Weekend–Easter
  Lunch daily, dinner Mon–Sat
Rest of year
  Lunch Tues–Sun, dinner Tues–Sat

Tasting **$5 per flight, refundable on purchase (cellar door or restaurant)**

Phone **06 873 7126**

Website **www.craggyrange.co.nz**

As monumental as the landscape it occupies, Craggy Range is a striking winery set on a wide river terrace above the Tukituki River and below Te Mata peak, though the winery actually takes its name from the range of hills across the river. Designed by architect John Blair, the winery style hints at the grand European chateau but retains a distinct New Zealand feel, and although large in scale Craggy Range still maintains a degree of intimacy with a small, formal courtyard garden and a spare but elegant tasting room.

The Terroir Restaurant is recognised as one of the best vineyard restaurants in the country, and as its name suggests combines all the natural elements to produce the best-quality dishes New Zealand has to offer.

Craggy Range takes pride in producing single-vineyard wines. Grapes are sourced from around the country and care is taken that the resulting wines retain their distinct regional flavours.

Kim Crawford Wines

Clifton Road
Te Awanga

Labels Kim Crawford
Crawford Farm

Specialisation Sauvignon Blanc
Chardonnay
Riesling
Merlot
Pinot Noir

Opening hours
Summer
Daily 11 am–6 pm
Winter
Sat/Sun/Mon 11 am–5 pm

Tasting Casual visitors no charge,
charge for groups

Phone 06 875 0553

Website
www.kimcrawfordwines.co.nz

Simple and stylish, this small cellar door at Te Awanga is set on a low rise with views over the vines to the sea, to Cape Kidnappers and beyond.

Although this is the public face of Kim Crawford, the company works with growers in Marlborough, Gisborne, Waipara and Central Otago as well as Hawke's Bay. The stony nature of the soil is very evident here, with pebbles and small rocks carefully heaped under the vines to assist with the ripening of the grapes.

Kim Crawford is strong on whites, including Sauvignon Blanc, Chardonnay, Riesling, Pinot Gris, Viognier and Gewürztraminer. Of the 40 wines the company entered in the 2006 Air New Zealand Awards, 30 won medals, including six golds, and a trophy for Champion Sauvignon Blanc.

In addition to wine tasting, Kim Crawford also has picnic facilities and apartment accommodation at Te Awanga.

Te Mata Estate

**349 Te Mata Road
Havelock North**

Labels **Te Mata
Woodthorpe**

Specialisation **Cabernet/Merlot
Syrah
Chardonnay**

Opening hours
**Mon–Fri 9 am–5 pm
Sat/public holidays 10 am–5 pm
Sun 11 am–4 pm**

Tasting **No charge**

Phone **06 877 4399**

Website **www.temata.co.nz**

Established in 1892, Te Mata is one of New Zealand's oldest vineyards; and although its fortunes varied throughout the twentieth century, in the late 1970s Te Mata again became the pin-up vineyard of the new generation of winemakers who have since made New Zealand wines internationally famous. The Ian Athfield-designed house so symbolic of that era is set among vines across the road from the current winery. What is often not realised is that Ian Athfield also designed the current winery building, using pale plaster and tiles to create something that has a classical feel and yet blends in with the older winery buildings. The entrance to the winery is over a small brick bridge, and is overhung by a huge old avocado tree and dominated by a roofless tower overgrown with ivy and leading to an elegant enclosed courtyard centred on tiled fish ponds.

With 10 vineyards scattered about Hawke's Bay, Te Mata produces a wide range of both red and white wines, from Syrah and Cabernet/Merlot to Chardonnay and Sauvignon Blanc. Te Mata's Woodthorpe wines come from a single vineyard of that name, and include Viognier and the unusual Gamay Noir made from the grape of Beaujolais.

Vidal was founded in 1905 by Spaniard Anthony Vidal. Just over 100 years later the winery is still going strong – in 2006 it won the New Zealand Winemaker of the Year Award at the Royal Easter Wine Show and at 2007's show picked up the Champion Viognier trophy.

Arriving from Spain in 1888 at the age of 22, Anthony Vidal first worked with his vintner uncle Joseph Soler in Wanganui. After a brief spell in Palmerston North, Anthony Vidal moved to Hawke's Bay in 1905, which he identified as a premium grape-growing district. With a passion to pursue winemaking he set about establishing vineyards and converted a stable into the winery which remains to this day. In addition to the vineyard in Hastings, he also planted grapes at Te Awanga and Te Mata, both now recognised as premium grape-growing districts.

While the vineyards around the Hastings winery have been swallowed up by urban expansion, and the winery is now part of the Villa Maria group, Vidal still retains a strong individuality, producing a wide range of award-winning red and white wines from grapes sourced from a variety of New Zealand vineyards. These include Hawke's Bay's famous Gimblett Gravels, a region capable of producing world-class red wines.

Vidal was also the first company to establish a winery restaurant, in 1979, with the restaurant, along with the tasting room, occupying the original winery stables. With their huge wooden wine barrels and historical photographs lining the wall, the old stables have a warm and welcoming ambience and are a popular dining spot for visitors and locals alike. With both indoor and courtyard dining, Vidal is open for lunch and dinner, with the menu focused on simple, fresh flavours. Alternatively, you can just relax with a glass or two in the wine bar.

Vidal Wines

913 St Aubyn Street East Hastings

Labels Vidal

Specialisation Chardonnay
Merlot/Cabernet
Syrah
Viogner

___

Opening hours
Daily
  10 am–5 pm winter
  10 am–6 pm summer
Restaurant daily for lunch
  and dinner

Tasting No charge
Phone 06 872 7441
Website www.vidal.co.nz

___

Zepelin

275 Te Mata Road
Havelock North

Labels **Zepelin**

Specialisation **Syrah**
Bordeaux-style blends
Rosé

Opening hours
Oct–Apr Sat/Sun/public holidays
10 am–5 pm

Tasting **$5, refundable on**
purchase

Phone **06 877 1477**

Website **www.zepelin.co.nz**

This name of this family-owned winery derives from the surname of current owner Ross Martin's grandfather, who immigrated to Australia and changed his name from Zepelin to Martin during World War I when things Germanic were distinctly out of favour (the Zeppelin airships are named after Count Von Zeppelin – with a double 'p').

Covering less than three hectares, this small vineyard on the outskirts of Havelock North specialises in and produces only red wines. While Zepelin has only recently opened a cellar door, the vineyard has been established for over 10 years and the current winemaker Malcolm Reeves has more than 25 years' experience working with Syrah.

There are brave vintners and very brave vintners, and Peter and Chris Hayward are very brave vintners. Located high above the sea on the Taranaki coast, Okurukuru has one of the most spectacular sites of any New Zealand vineyard, but what a hard place to grow grapes. Exposed to the prevailing westerly winds and receiving high rainfall, the lush climate of Taranaki is a test to any grape grower, but Okurukuru have planted Pinotage, Pinot Gris and Pinot Noir and in 2006 produced their first vintage with a Taranaki Rosé. In addition the range is supplemented with Marlborough-sourced grapes producing Sauvignon Blanc, Pinot Noir and Chardonnay.

Okurukuru have taken full advantage of a stunning site by building a modern and very stylish restaurant accentuating views both of the coastline and of the mountain. Blending into the hillside and imitating an ocean wave, the building's extensive use of huge glass windows ensures a view in every direction. Whether it is for weekend brunch, lunch, dinner, coffee and cake or just a relaxing glass of wine, Okurukuru is not to be missed in any visit to Taranaki.

The winery hosts the Taranaki Wine and Food Festival (www.taranakiwineandfood.com) in March each year.

Okurukuru Wines

738 Surf Highway 45 Omata

Labels Okurukuru

Specialisation Rosé
Sauvignon Blanc

Opening hours
Tues–Sun from 9 am

Tasting No charge
Phone 06 751 0787
Website www.thevineyard.co.nz

Pohangina Valley Estate

1034 Pohangina Valley Road
30 minutes from Palmerston North

Labels Pohangina Estate

Specialisation Pinot Gris
Pinot Noir

Opening hours
Oct–Dec Sun only 11 am–4.30 pm
Jan–Apr Sat/Sun 11 am–4.30 pm

Tasting Casual visitors no charge, groups by appointment

Phone 06 354 7948

Website www.yellow.co.nz/site/pohanginavalleyestate

The only vineyard in the Manawatu, Pohangina Valley Estate is set on an old, stony, river terrace in this very picturesque valley. The fertile Pohangina Valley lies to the west of the bush-clad Ruahine ranges and being sheltered can be very warm in summer, though in an exceptional winter, a heavy snow fall is not uncommon. The small vineyard of Pinot Gris, Pinot Noir and Chardonnay grapes was planted in 2000 and 2001, with the first vintage in 2004. Pinot Gris from that year won a silver medal in the Cuisine Awards in 2005, and they have won an award for every vintage since their inception.

A family business, the vineyard is part of a working farm and, as well as grapes, olive trees and truffles are planned to come on-line in the future. The wine is currently produced in Martinborough, but a small, friendly tasting room is open on the weekends and is well worth the short drive from Palmerston North.

The Taste of Taranaki

While fruit wineries are beyond the scope of this book, Sentry Hill just outside New Plymouth produces an excellent Traditional Green Ginger wine. Green ginger wine has a long history and grew in popularity in the eighteenth and nineteenth centuries as prevention for cholera; today, ginger still has a reputation as a good aid for digestion and other stomach ailments.

In addition to green ginger wine Sentry Hill produces a number of award-winning fruit wines and is a very friendly small winery that is well worth a visit.

Sentry Hill Winery

152 Cross Road Lepperton, Taranaki

Labels **Sentry Hill**

Specialisation **Fruit wines**

Opening hours
Oct–Mar Mon–Fri 11 am–3 pm
Apr–Sep Thurs/Fri 11 am–3 pm
All year Sat/Sun/public holidays
10 am–4pm

Tasting **No charge**
Phone **06 752 0778**
Website
www.sentryhillwinery. co.nz

Sulphur dioxide (SO$_2$)

In modern winemaking, sulphur dioxide is added to newly picked grapes to prevent premature fermentation, to newly fermenting wine, to barrels in which wine is stored, and to wine in discreet doses to act as a preservative. Used in moderation it imparts no taste or aroma.

Alana Estate

**Puruatanga Road
Martinborough**

Labels **Alana Estate**

Specialisation **Chardonnay
Pinot Noir**

Opening hours
**Daily 10.30 am–5 pm
Lunch 11 am–3.30 pm
Dinner Sat only**

Tasting **Casual visitors no charge,
groups small charge**

Phone **06 306 9784**

Website **www.alana.co.nz**

With the opening of its restaurant in 2005, and one of the few Martinborough wineries open seven days a week all year round, Alana has within a few short years become one of most popular destinations on the Martinborough wine trail.

Located on the edge of the famous Martinborough Terrace above the Huangarua River, Alana is strong on Chardonnay with a reputation for consistent quality, and in 2001 its Pinot Noir was one of just 12 chosen to represent New Zealand on the international stage. In addition Alana produces an excellent Methode Traditionelle, and a tasty Late Harvest Riesling. This gravity-fed winery (which reduces the level of damage to the grapes during processing) places a high value on quality, and many of Alana's best wines are available only from the cellar door.

The restaurant menu offers good fresh food, simply prepared and with wines to match, with comfortable indoor dining, and a beautiful wide terrace in the summer. Their venison burger is particularly popular especially when matched with older-vintage Pinot Noir.

Alana hosts the occasional vineyard concerts, and the Molenberg/Sub60 vineyard run/walk as well as other events.

Ata Rangi is the winemakers' vineyard, the one winery that other winemakers consistently say that they want to visit. Established in 1980, Ata Rangi is one of the area's earliest vineyards, and from an original five-hectare block Ata Rangi now has 30 hectares under vines nearly all within one kilometre of the winery. All the grapes for its famous Pinot Noir are sourced from Martinborough, and over 25 years later many of the original vines are still producing wines that are consistently recognised as top of their class.

The reviews and awards for Ata Rangi's wines are almost endless. In particular the Pinot Noir is internationally recognised as one of New Zealand's best, but the Chardonnay and Riesling are not to be forgotten. The small tasting room is simple and stylish and in summer air-conditioned, a perfect spot on a hot Wairarapa summer's afternoon!

Ata Rangi

Puruatanga Road
Martinborough

Labels **Ata Rangi**

Specialisation **Pinot Noir**
Chardonnay
Pinot Gris

Opening hours
Sept
   Sat/Sun 12 noon–4 pm
Oct–Easter
   Mon–Fri 1–3 pm
   Sat/Sun 12 noon–4 pm

Tasting **$2 per tasting, refunded on purchase**

Phone **06 306 9570**

Website **www.atarangi.co.nz**

Benfield and Delamare

35 New York Street
Martinborough

Labels **Benfield and Delamare**

Specialisation **Merlot**
Cabernet Sauvignon

Opening hours
1 Oct–1 May Sat/Sun 1 pm–5 pm

Tasting **No charge**
Phone **06 306 9926**

Website
www.benfieldanddelamare.co.nz

This small boutique winery, virtually in town, covers just two and a half hectares, and while having a primary focus on red wine also produces a very limited number of cases of white. Established in 1987 by Bill Benfield and Sue Delamare, the vineyard's grapes are grown low to the ground, are not irrigated and are hand-picked and basket-crushed with all the processes carried out in a tiny winery. Equally tiny is the cosy tasting room that also doubles as the office and the lab! Producing consistently good wine since 1990 (both first vintages won gold awards), Benfield and Delamare wines have a very limited distribution through selected outlets — the winemakers have deliberately refused to print a barcode on their label, thereby preventing the wine from being sold in more mass-market outlets.

Fortified wines

Fortified wines are those to which brandy has been added to stop fermentation and increase alcohol content. Made from either white or red grapes, they range from dry sherries (e.g. Fino, Manzanilla) through to sweet sherries (e.g Cream, Oporto) and port. Other fortified styles are Marsala (from Sicily), Madeira (from Portugal) and the fortified Muscats and Tokays (from Australia).

Part of the 'second wave' in Martinborough, Coney Wines has just three vintages, including Riesling, Pinot Noir and Rosé, all given distinctive music-related names such as Ragtime Riesling and Pizzicato Pinot Noir. However, what Margaret and Tim Coney may lack in experience, they certainly make up for with personal enthusiasm and charm. In addition to the vineyard they have also established an excellent restaurant where Margaret is dedicated to preparing tasty café-style dishes from the best local ingredients, while Tim entertainingly takes charge of the wine tasting and vineyard work. Open for lunch during the weekend only, the setting of Coney Wines is just lovely. During summer tables are set out around a small, north-facing courtyard with views across the Wairarapa plain out towards the rugged ranges of the Tararuas. The vine-entwined loggia protects the diners from the heat of the sun, while in winter an open fireplace has its own warmth. What's more the prices are, by vineyard standards, very reasonable.

Coney Wines

Dry River Road
Martinborough

Labels **Coney**

Specialisation **Riesling**
Pinot Noir

Opening hours
Sat/Sun/public holidays
11 am–5 pm, including café;
evenings, groups only
Closed Aug/Sept

Tasting **Casual visitors no charge**
Phone **06 306 8345**
Website **www.coneywines.co.nz**

Gladstone Vineyard

Gladstone Road
Carterton

Labels Gladstone
          12,000 Miles

Specialisation Sauvignon Blanc
                Pinot Gris
                Pinot Noir

Opening hours
Tues–Sun, public holidays (Mon)
  11 am–5 pm
  Closed Christmas, Boxing and
  New Year's Days, Good Friday
Café
  Fri–Sun, public holidays (Mon)
  11 am–3 pm

Tasting Charge for groups
Phone 06 379 8563
Website www.gladstone.co.nz

While the focus of grape-growing in the Wairarapa is on Martinborough, in recent years attention has been shifting to the Gladstone area to the north. Like its more southerly counterpart, the area's vineyards are located on stony, well-drained river terraces of the Ruamahanga River, and with low rainfall produce low-cropping but intensely flavoured grapes.

Gladstone Vineyard was established in 1986, and has expanded to 14 hectares, producing a wide range of white and red wines including Pinot Gris, Sauvignon Blanc, Viognier, Pinot Noir, Rosé and a Bordeaux-style wine labelled Auld Alliance. The attractive winery is modern and stylish and set among trees and gardens in the heart of the vineyard. The old winery has been converted into Stokers, a café with indoor dining in the old barrel room and outdoor dining on an open terrace overlooking the vineyard and gardens. Open for lunch or just a glass of wine, the setting is relaxed and a children's playground has been provided to keep the younger ones occupied.

Situated just north of Masterton, Loopline is the most northerly of the Wairarapa vineyards and receives higher rainfall and less sun than further south. Located on an old riverbed, with thin topsoil lying over gravel, the vineyard produces a surprising seven varieties of wine from just four hectares, including Riesling, Sauvignon Blanc, Chardonnay, Pinot Gris, Cabernet, Merlot and Pinot Noir. Loopline grapes are hand-picked and all the processes are carried out in the small winery; the wine is available only from the cellar door and local outlets. It is small, friendly and well worth a short detour off State Highway 2. Unlike many of the Wairarapa vineyards, Loopline is open seven days a week.

Loopline Vineyard

37 Loop Line, Opaki Masterton

Labels Loopline

Specialisation Pinot Gris
Riesling

Opening hours
Daily 10 am–5 pm

Tasting **Casual visitors no charge, groups small charge**

Phone **06 377 3353**

Website **www.loopline.co.nz**

Margrain Vineyard

Cnr Ponatahi and
Huangarua Roads
Martinborough

Labels Margrain

Specialisation Pinot Noir
Gewürztraminer
Chenin Blanc

Opening hours
All year 11 am–5 pm; Sat/Sun
Dec–Easter Fri/Sat/Sun
Jan daily

Tasting $5 per person, refundable
on purchase

Phone 06 306 9292

Website
www.margrainvineyard.co.nz

Like most Martinborough vineyards, family-owned Margrain is strong on Pinot Noir, but produces a wide range of wines including Sauvignon Blanc, Riesling, Pinot Gris, Pinot Rosé, Chardonnay and, unusually for the Wairarapa, Gewürztraminer and Chenin Blanc also. All Margrain's wines are from grapes grown in the area, hand-picked and carefully processed to ensure the best quality.

The Old Winery Café at Margrain serves excellent, simple food in a very relaxed atmosphere alongside the vineyard, with wines carefully matched to the food on the menu. Just down the road next to the actual winery, Margrain provides conference facilities and very stylish accommodation designed by architect Roger Walker.

Established in 1980, Martinborough Vineyard was one of the first four vineyards in the Martinborough area, following a 1978 government report which identified this area as the New Zealand climate most similar to that of Burgundy in France. Derek Milne, one of the report's authors, was so enthusiastic about the prospect of growing grapes and producing world-class wines here that he and four others purchased land and established Martinborough Vineyard.

The entrance to this charming winery is through a formal rose garden and verandas overhung with wisteria to a pleasant, friendly tasting room looking out to the vineyard. Visitors are welcome to bring a picnic.

While best known for their Pinot Noir which has won numerous awards, Martinborough also have an extensive range of whites including Riesling, Chardonnay, Sauvignon Blanc and Pinot Gris.

Martinborough Vineyard

Princess Street
Martinborough

Labels Martinborough Vineyard
Burnt Spur

Specialisation Pinot Noir

Opening hours
Mon–Fri 10 am–3 pm
Sat/Sun 10 am–5 pm

Tasting $5 per person, refundable on purchase

Phone 06 306 9955

Website www.martinborough-vineyard.co.nz

Murdoch James

**Dry River Road
Martinborough**

Labels Murdoch James

Specialisation Pinot Noir
Syrah
Unoaked Chardonnay

Opening hours
Daily 11 am–5 pm daily (closed
Christmas and New Year's Days)
Café 11.30 am–3.30 pm
Apr–Oct, Fri–Sun
Nov–Mar, Thurs–Mon
(closed over Christmas)

Tasting $5 for six wines

Phone 06 306 9165

Website
www.murdochjames.co.nz

Along with Coney Wines (see page 89), Murdoch James is about nine kilometres out of Martinborough, and certainly well worth the trip. Alongside the actual Dry River (which seasonally has water flowing along its stony river bed), Murdoch James is perched above the river with the barrel room dug deep into the cool hillside under the winery and terraced restaurant. Like all Wairarapa vineyards Pinot Noir dominates, but the windy and exposed nature of these grape vines results in a lighter crop with more distinct flavours. However, don't underestimate the Rieslings from this area. This variety makes up the greater percentage of wine exported from Murdoch James.

In addition to growing grapes, Murdoch James offers specialised wine-appreciation tours. The more comprehensive ones are usually by appointment, but there is a set tour at 11.30 (called 'From Grape To Glass') which moves from the vineyard to the winery and then to the cellars, tasting all the way, every Saturday and Sunday (bookings preferred).

The Riverview Café has dramatic views of the Wairarapa plain and out to the Tararua ranges, and offers a good range of food with a distinct New Zealand flavour at reasonable prices; while for those wanting a picnic there are great spots under large shade trees by a pond.

Sitting on a rise on the main road into Martinborough from the north, Palliser Estate winery has successfully produced award-winning wines across all of its varietals since 1990. Its 2006 Riesling, off-dry style, won Gold at the Air New Zealand Awards 2006 and also received the Champion Riesling trophy.

The winery is accommodated in modern buildings reminiscent of old stables bordering a sheltered courtyard, creating a pleasant quiet place for a picnic and to enjoy wine tasting.

Palliser Estate

Kitchener Street
Martinborough

Labels **Palliser Estate**
      Pencarrow

Specialisation **Pinot Noir**
            Sauvignon Blanc
            Riesling

Opening hours
**Daily 10.30 am–4 pm, and to 5 pm
Sat/Sun during daylight saving**

Tasting **$4 per person**
Phone **06 306 9019**
Website **www.palliser.co.nz**

Schubert Wines

57 Cambridge Road
Martinborough

Labels Schubert

Specialisation Pinot Noir
Cabernet/Merlot

Opening hours
Daily 11 am–3 pm

Tasting Casual visitors no charge

Phone **06 306 8505**

Website **www.schubert.co.nz**

Newcomers to the Martinborough area, German viti-culturalist Kai Schubert and partner Marion Deimling acquired a small, established vineyard in 1998, releasing their first vintage in 2001 and their first Pinot Noir in 2003. While Pinot Noir makes up 75% of Schubert's 12 hectares, another speciality of this winery is Tribianco, a blend of Chardonnay, Pinot Gris and Müller-Thurgau — the ideal wine to have with spicy Asian food. In fact, Asia is a significant export destination for Schubert wines.

The tasting room might be tiny, but here you are very likely to have the winemaker himself guide you through the tasting.

Like many Martinborough wineries Te Kairanga has a reputation for Pinot Noir sourced from grapes from its six local vineyards on the famous Martinborough Terrace. Its Syrah is from Hawke's Bay grapes and the Merlot from Gisborne. Te Kairanga white wines include Chardonnay, Sauvignon Blanc and Riesling, and helpful tasting notes are provided.

The winery and home blocks are located on the original land of Martinborough's founder John Martin and the tasting room is his head stockman's cottage, built 130 years ago (the poet Sam Hunt also lived in the cottage at one stage). Set among broad lawns and mature trees, this is an excellent spot to relax with a picnic lunch and glass or two of wine under the trees on a warm summer's day. Platter food is also available.

Te Kairanga

Martins Road
Martinborough

Labels Te Kairanga

Specialisation Pinot Noir
Chardonnay

Opening hours
Daily from 10 am

Tasting No charge for casual
visitors

Phone 06 306 9122

Website www.tekairanga.co.nz

Tirohana Estate

**Puruatanga Road
Martinborough**

Labels Tirohana

Specialisation Pinot Noir
Dessert wines

Opening hours
Daily 9 am–6 pm
Closed Christmas Day, Good
  Friday and Anzac Day morning

Tasting $1 per wine tasted

Phone 06 306 9933

Website www.tirohanaestate.com

Located in the heart of Martinborough's wine country, Tirohana is a delightful family-owned vineyard with all the charm and none of the pretension. All their wines are sourced from this one vineyard, and unusually Tirohana do not blend their wines. As well as their Pinot Noir, their dessert wine Noble Spirit is also highly recommended.

The friendly tasting room also offers a range of wine jellies, chutneys and preserves. Visitors are welcome to bring a picnic, or arrange for Tirohana to provide a pre-packed picnic lunch. Tirohana also offers five-star accommodation.

jm Tarnock Photography

Allan Scott

Jacksons Road
Blenheim

Labels **Allan Scott**

Specialisation **Sauvignon Blanc**
Riesling
Pinot Gris
Gewürztraminer

Opening hours
**Daily 9 am–5 pm except
Christmas, Boxing, New Year's
Day, Anzac Day, Good Friday**

Tasting **$2 per wine, refundable
on purchase**

Phone **03 572 9054**

Website **www.allanscott.com**

One of Marlborough's most popular vineyards, family-owned Allan Scott has consistently produced good wines and run one of the best vineyard restaurants in the region. All its wines are from Marlborough, and in fact come exclusively from the Rapaura area very close to the winery. Under the Allan Scott label there are two ranges: the estate range which is blended, and the prestige range which are all single-vineyard wines. The latter is not widely available beyond the Allan Scott cellar door and restaurant.

The vineyard is long-established, with the first grapes planted in 1973 and the winery open since 1990; 2006 is the winery's 30th vintage. Some of the vines here are among the oldest in Marlborough, with some Riesling vines over 30 years old and still going strong. The winery produces a sparkling wine called Blanc de Blancs produced from 100% Chardonnay grapes, as well as a sparkling Rosé Cuvée and a Pinot Rosé.

The restaurant is deservedly popular and bookings are essential during the busy summer months. Set in a delightful courtyard, the restaurant strikes a neat balance between formal and relaxed, with topiary, warm rustic tiles and wood, fountains and a herb garden. Don't be surprised to see a chef rushing madly through the diners to pick fresh herbs for a dish under way in the kitchen. There is a giant chess set for those wanting a more intellectual challenge between glasses of good wine. The food is cooked in the emerging modern New Zealand style, with a seasonal emphasis on fresh local produce overlaid with Asian and Mediterranean influences.

The Scott family are now providing a second generation of winemakers; and across the road son Josh Scott brews Moa Beer in a microbrewery, which is open for tastings during the summer months and available at the cellar door and in the restaurant.

Bladen Wines

**Conders Bend Road
Renwick**

Labels **Bladen**

Specialisation **Pinot Gris
Gewürztraminer**

Opening hours
**Labour Weekend–Easter
daily 11 am–5 pm**

Tasting **No charge**

Phone **03 572 9417**

Website **www.bladen.co.nz**

This vineyard of only eight hectares may be small, but it has a string of almost 200 awards for its aromatics, including the 2004 Royal Easter Show Wine Gold for its Pinot Gris. Planted in 1989 and with its first vintage in 1997, the vineyard's grapes are mainly hand-harvested and are all single-vineyard wines, with the exception of the Sauvignon Blanc which is produced from solely Marlborough fruit.

The tiny tasting room, no more than a hole in the wall, is reached down a bumpy driveway, but the service at the end is very friendly and personal and there is every chance you will meet the owners and winemaker.

Cloudy Bay

Cloudy Bay is one of most internationally recognised New Zealand wine labels and probably the one label that established Sauvignon Blanc as a leading New World wine on the global wine stage. While Sauvignon Blanc is this winery's best-known wine, it also produces a wide range of excellent vintages including Chardonnay, Pinot Noir, Riesling, wild-fermented Sauvignon Blanc, Gewürztraminer, Pinot Gris, late harvest Riesling and sparkling wine (both vintage and non-vintage, under the Pelorus label). Production speed and maintenance of quality has been the key to success for Cloudy Bay's Sauvignon Blanc — as well as the knowledge that no winery can base future success on past accolades and must ensure that each vintage produces the very best wine.

The tasting room is simple and stylish and is surrounded by large eucalypts reflecting the Australian origins of David Honen, who along with winemaker Kevin Judd established Cloudy Bay as a leading producer of Sauvignon Blanc. The view from the vineyard of the rugged Richmond Ranges is reflected on the winery's label, and planted around the winery is Sauvignon Blanc, the very variety that has made this winery so very famous.

Needless to say, this winery is very popular, and varieties and vintages can sell out very fast. However, Cloudy Bay ensures that each new vintage is available at the cellar door first and often has vintages and varieties there that are not available elsewhere.

Jacksons Road
Blenheim

Labels **Cloudy Bay**
Pelorus

Specialisation **Sauvignon Blanc**
Sparkling wine
Pinot Noir
Chardonnay

Opening hours
Daily 10 am–5 pm
Closed Christmas Day, Good
Friday

Tasting **No charge, but groups**
by appointment only
Phone **03 520 9140**
Website **www.cloudybay.co.nz**

Domaine Georges Michel

56 Vintage Lane
Blenheim (near Renwick)

Labels Domaine Georges Michel

Specialisation Chardonnay
Sauvignon Blanc
Pinot Noir

Opening hours
Labour Weekend–Easter
Tues–Sun 10 am–4.30 pm
Rest of year 11 am–4 pm
Restaurant 10 am–3 pm

Tasting **No charge**
Phone **03 572 7230**
Website
www.georgesmichel.co.nz

Established in 1997, this European-influenced boutique winery produces wines from three Marlborough vineyards and, in addition to Chardonnay and Pinot Noir, Rosé and Sauvignon Blanc, includes a dessert wine (a Sauvignon Blanc/Semillon blend) and Marc, a grappa-type spirit that is oak-aged. Domaine Georges Michel produces New Zealand-style wines under the Golden Mile range (which refers to the 'golden mile' of vineyards along Rapaura Road) and, under the La Reserve name, European-style wines in much smaller quantities, reflecting the French origin of Georges Michel who still owns Chateau de Grandmont in Burgundy. The European influence is further strengthened by wine consultant Guy Brac de la Perrière, who comes from a long line of French winemakers and who oversees the winemaking process.

Pacific Rim flavours are the focus of the restaurant, which is open during the day for casual dining, from a cup of coffee or a glass of wine through to lunch with tasting platters available at any time. The small shop at the cellar door also sells a range of French wines selected by Georges, along with olive oil and a range of crafts.

Making just four wines from a single vineyard, this family-owned winery focuses on quality and produces its wines from the best of the harvest, selling off the balance. Established in 1982, Fairhall Downs sits a surprising 90 metres above sea level; the small Cape Dutch-inspired tasting room is located on a high terrace with the Wither Hills rising like a painting behind the vineyard, making this one of the most attractively located vineyards in the Marlborough area.

Fairhall Downs

**70 Wrekin Road
Brancott Valley
Blenheim**

Labels Fairhall Downs

Specialisation Sauvignon Blanc
Pinot Gris
Chardonnay
Pinot Noir

Opening hours
Mon–Fri 9 am–4 pm

Tasting No charge
Phone 03 572 8356
Website www.fairhalldowns.co.nz

Forrest Estate Winery

19 Blicks Road (off SH 6) Renwick

Labels Forrest Estate

Specialisation Bordeaux-style reds
Riesling
Botrytis Riesling

Opening hours
Daily 10 am–4.30 pm
except Christmas, Boxing and
New Year's Days, Marlborough
Anniversary, Good Friday

Tasting $5 per person for
six wines

Phone 03 572 9084

Website www.forrestwines.co.nz

Forrest Estate
has long been a
sponsor of cycling,
supporting both
the Lake Brunner
Ride and its own
102-km Grape
Ride, the latter
both beginning
and ending in
the vineyard and
attracting over 1000
cyclists (see www.
graperide.com).

Unusually for Marlborough vineyards, family-owned Forrest Estate sources grapes from six vineyards around the country, including Hawke's Bay, North Otago (Waitaki Valley) and Central Otago, enabling the winery to offer a broad range of wines for tasting. Its Cornerstone Bordeaux-style blend comes from grapes grown on the famous Gimblett Gravels of the Hawke's Bay, while from Marlborough comes a range of Rieslings that is second to none. Forrest is the only South Island producer of Chenin Blanc.

The winery, surrounded by vines of Sauvignon Blanc, is a particularly popular family picnic spot with spacious grounds of lawns, ponds and large shade trees. Through the gardens and along the long drive leading into the winery are modern sculptured art works, and during the summer you can watch the sculptor Timothy Mark at work. The large tasting room has plenty of space to spread out in, both outdoors in the summer and by the cosy fire in winter. With such a broad range of wines on offer, including Sauvignon Blanc, Riesling, Gewürztraminer, dry Rosé, Syrah, Pinot Noir, Merlot Malbec and Cabernet Sauvignon/Merlot/Malbec, Forrest offers a tasting tray of six wines from a list of 16 types to be enjoyed in the sun or by the fire.

Taking its name from the English village where the owner's grandfather came from, this boutique vineyard has as its motto 'Classic by name, classic by reputation'. And it is spot-on. From the entrance-way through the formal courtyard of lavender and roses, entering Framingham's is like walking into an English gentlemen's club or country pub. The walls are wood-panelled, the chairs deep and leather-covered, while wine antiques and rows of older vintages find a home down in the stylish barrel room. On the wall hangs a copy of a large 15th century French tapestry 'Les Vendages', the original of which hangs in the Musée de Cluny in Paris. And even the ceramic handbasins in the women's toilets, made by a Nelson potter, have a reputation all of their own — making these the women's toilets most visited by men in the country.

But Framingham is not all about the 'old country'. Its smart label reflects both European and Maori heritage; the carving on which the label is based hangs on the wall behind the counter in the tasting room.

Riesling drives their reputation as winemakers with four different types of Riesling on offer, plus a dessert Riesling which has attracted several awards. The Riesling block in front of the winery is one of the oldest in the Wairau Valley. In addition to Pinot Noir, Framingham's Montepulciano has a local cult following, and all their wines are from grapes sourced in Marlborough.

Framingham Wine Company

Conders Bend Road
Renwick

Labels **Framingham**

Specialisation **Riesling**
Sauvignon Blanc

Opening hours
Daily 11 am–4 pm

Tasting **No charge**

Phone **03 572 8884**

Website **www.framingham.co.nz**

Fromm Winery
La Strada

Godfrey Road
Blenheim (near Renwick)

Labels **Fromm**
      La Strada
      Clayvin Vineyard

Specialisation **Pinot Noir**

Opening hours
Labour Weekend–Easter
  daily 11 am–5 pm
Rest of year
  Fri–Sun 11 am–4 pm

Tasting   Casual visitors no charge,
        small charge for groups
        over 10

Phone   **03 572 9355**

Website
www.frommwineries.com

This respected winery has a deserved reputation for producing distinctive wines in the European style which, unlike most New Zealand wines, are made not only to be drunk fresh but also have excellent cellaring qualities. On just five hectares from two Marlborough vineyards, Fromm produces a surprising range of wines from low-cropping and intensely flavoured fruit. As well as four types of Pinot Noir, it produces one of the country's best Chardonnays, a fresh low-alcohol Riesling (just 7.5%), Syrah, Malbec, a single-vineyard Merlot and a late harvest Gewürztraminer.

The vineyard is owned by Swiss couple George Fromm and Pol Lenzinger, who have a long family tradition of winemaking, and the winery itself is also Swiss-designed. All the processes are carried out on their premises and there is a view into the winery and barrel room from the tasting area.

A tiny vineyard of just two hectares, Gibson Bridge has just one vintage to date, a very credible Pinot Gris, with Gewürztraminer and a blended red planned for the future. With a strong focus on quality, Gibson Bridge reduces grape yield by almost half to ensure only the best grapes are harvested. The small tasting room with its beautiful timber workbench has been built by the owner, who also hand-planted all the vines. Gibson Bridge Pinot Gris is available only from the cellar door and selected local restaurants.

Gibson Bridge

Cnr Gee Street and Nelson Highway (SH 6) Renwick

Labels **Gibson Bridge**

Specialisation **Pinot Gris**

Opening hours
Daily 10 am–3 pm

Tasting **No charge**
Phone **03 572 5180**

Basket press

Before the advent of modern winemaking, most presses were basket presses made of wood and operated manually. The 'basket' is a cylinder of wooden slats on top of a fixed base with a moveable plate that can be screwed downwards. Today a basket press is mainly used for small pressings of grapes from an exceptional vintage.

Grove Mill

Waihopai Valley Road
Renwick

Labels **Grove Mill**
Sanctuary

Specialisation **Riesling**
Pinot Gris

Opening hours
Daily 11 am–5 pm

Tasting **No charge**
Phone **03 575 8200**
Website **www.grovemill.co.nz**

In an area dominated by Sauvignon Blanc, the winemaker at Grove Mill has a strong reputation for excellent Riesling – which was the very first type of wine that Grove Mill produced in 1988. Since then Pinot Noir, Pinot Gris, Sauvignon Blanc, Chardonnay and Gewürztraminer have been added to its range.

In addition to wine tasting Grove Mill has a unique 'Grape Library', where in autumn it is possible to taste the grapes from which different varieties of wine are made and compare the taste of the grape to the finished wine. The library is part of a test vineyard alongside the winery. Grove Mill also offers an aroma demonstration, though this must be booked ahead, and the tasting room is also part art gallery with works by leading New Zealand artists for sale.

The vineyard has a pleasant picnic area alongside a restored wetland planted with over 4000 native plants, some of which are labelled to assist with identification. This reflects the strong environmental focus present since the winery was established, and now Grove Mill is actively pursuing a carbon-zero programme, taking great pride in being the only carbon-neutral winery in the country.

Champagne or Methode Traditionelle/Methode Champenoise

The only wine with any right to the name 'champagne' is that made from legally specified grapes grown in limited and defined sections of the province in France called Champagne. The champagne process is the 'traditional method' of making wine sparkle by allowing it to ferment a second time in the bottle. If it fizzes but is not from Champagne, then it is sparkling wine.

Sparkling wines are those that are made effervescent by the presence of carbon dioxide in the bottle. The best are made using the champagne method of secondary fermentation in the bottle. The others are made either by the bulk process of fermenting in tanks and bottling under pressure (charmat method), or by adding carbon dioxide as you would find in fizzy drinks (carbonated wines).

A small vineyard of only 11 hectares with a total of 3000 cases per year, Herzog produces a surprising array of wines that doesn't include Sauvignon Blanc, but *does* include Pinot Noir, Pinot Gris, Viognier, Chardonnay, Montepulciano, Pinot Rosé, Merlot/Cabernet Sauvignon, sparkling Rosé, Nebbiolo and dessert wine. First planted in 1994, the vineyard runs down to the Wairau River and is densely planted but with low yields producing quality fruit. All the processes are completed on-site and Herzog is biodynamic and sustainable in its vineyard practices. Many of its wines are available only through the cellar door or restaurant, including small quantities of older vintages.

However, it is fair to say that the restaurant is more widely known and recognised than Herzog's wines, and is consistently cited as New Zealand's finest restaurant. Hans and Theresa Herzog developed the food side of the business with the same dedication, passion and flair that they apply to their wines. A destination restaurant, the emphasis is on seasonal and market-fresh produce. As such the menu changes very regularly and is even tweaked on a daily basis to match the food available. The wine selection is extraordinary, with the very best of New Zealand and international wines sourced from over 600 labels. As well as a fine wine list there is a superb range of cigars, liqueurs, ports, brandies and cognacs. This of course comes at a price, and a night at Herzog's is not for the financially faint-hearted. However, more accessible is the bistro, serving lunches with a focus on a lighter seasonal mix. For real foodies, Herzog also runs cooking master-classes given by their Michelin-star-rated team.

Herzog Winery and Restaurant

**81 Jeffries Road
Blenheim (near Renwick)**

Labels **Herzog**

Specialisation **Pinot Gris
Viognier
Chardonnay**

Opening hours
All year
  Mon–Fri 9 am–5 pm
Oct–May
  also Sat/Sun 11 am–4 pm
Restaurant
  Oct–May Tues–Sun from 6.30 pm
Bistro
  Tues–Sun 12 noon–3 pm

Tasting **No charge**
Phone **03 572 8770**
Website **www.herzog.co.nz**

Highfield Estate

**Brookby Road
Omaka Valley
Blenheim**

Labels Highfield

Specialisation Elstree sparkling wine
Sauvignon Blanc

Opening hours
**Daily 10 am–5 pm
Restaurant 11 am–3.30 pm**

Tasting **Casual visitors no charge,
small charge for groups**

Phone **03 572 9244**

Website **www.highfield.co.nz**

Winner of the inaugural Best Cellar Door Award in 2007, Highfield has long been a popular destination for both visitors and locals alike, and at just four hectares is one of the smaller vineyards in the region.

Designed in the distinct faux 'bella Tuscany' style by architect and former Wellington mayor Michael Fowler, the building at Highfield is set on Brookby ridge above the Wairau Valley and was inspired by an actual Tuscan building called Capaggiolo. From the tower the views are superb, complemented by a photographic panorama highlighting the main landscape features such as Mt Richmond, The Patriarch, Mt Baldy and, in the far distance across the strait, the clearly visible North Island.

Using only Marlborough-grown grapes, Highfield produces Chardonnay, Pinot Noir, Riesling, Botrytis Riesling, the respected sparkling wine Elstree Marlborough Cuvée Brut and, of course, Sauvignon Blanc. As well as wine Highfield produces its own olive oil and home-made dukka.

Like the tower, the restaurant enjoys fine views and produces food in a broad Mediterranean style with a strong emphasis on local produce. As well as indoor dining Highfield has a lovely, broad terrace overlooking rows of Pinot Noir grapes with additional tables set among the vines in summer — just the spot to enjoy the popular summer platters and a glass of wine or two. If you are feeling frisky then a pétanque court is handy, or you can shop for gifts from a select range of vine-related merchandise including the immensely popular pearl necklaces formed in the shape of a bunch of grapes. A new addition to the food range is the Oyster Bar where the shellfish are freshly shucked when in season. And if all this is not enough, Highfield also offers accommodation so you never have to leave!

Rightfully described as a Marlborough icon, Hunter's is a popular destination winery, not least because of the owner, the irrepressible Jane Hunter. Jane has received both an MBE and an honorary doctorate for her contribution to New Zealand viticulture, and was the inaugural winner of the international 'Women In Wine Award'.

Established in 1983 by Ernie and Jane Hunter, Hunter's has now won more than 100 gold medals for its wine, in particular its outstanding Sauvignon Blanc. In addition to tasting their wines, Hunter's offer relaxed dining for both lunch and dinner in their comfortable restaurant, an artist in residence, Clarry Neemes, and an extensive native garden surrounding the winery that reflects the hardy plants of the dry Wairau Valley. Scattered throughout the garden are contemporary New Zealand works of art.

As well as grapes, Hunter's also grows olives and produces fine oils and marinated olives, all made on the property, along with tapenade and dukka.

Botrytis cinerea (noble rot)

Botrytis is a parasitic fungus or mould that attacks grapes. In certain climates the grapes will rot and spoil, while in others Botrytis cinerea or 'noble rot' can produce the greatest sweet wines in the world. The fungal infection removes water from the grapes leaving behind higher sugar levels, resulting in a more intense and concentrated product. Specific types include Sauternes, Monbazillac and Anjou from France; Auslese, Beerenauslese and Trockenbeerenauslese from Germany; and Tokay from Hungary.

Hunter's Wines

Rapaura Road
Blenheim

Labels Hunter's
        Miru Miru
        Kaharoa
        Hukapapa

Specialisation Sauvignon Blanc
                Sparkling wine
                (Miru Miru)

Opening hours
Daily 9.30 am–4.30 pm
Restaurant
  Lunch
    Labour Weekend–Easter
      11.30 am–3 pm
    Rest of year
      12 noon–2.30 pm
  Dinner from 6 pm

Tasting Casual visitors no charge,
         charge for groups
Phone   03 572 8489

Website www.hunters.co.nz

Isabel Estate Vineyard

**72 Hawkesbury Road
Renwick**

Labels **Isabel**

Specialisation **Sauvignon Blanc
Pinot Noir**

Opening hours
1 Dec–1 Apr approx.
  Mon–Sat 11 am–4 pm
Rest of year
  Mon–Fri 11 am–4 pm

Tasting **No charge**

Phone **03 572 8300**

Website **www.isabelestate.com**

Isabel Estate is owned by Mike and Robyn Tiller. Mike was originally a pilot, and on one of his regular flights into Blenheim noticed a piece of land that was consistently more frost-free than the surrounding land. This became Isabel Estate, named after Mike's mum. One of the earlier vineyards in the area, the first grapes were planted in 1982; they were also early planters of Pinot Noir in 1994. All the wines are from hand-picked grapes off this one block and all the processes are carried out at the Isabel winery. In addition to their Sauvignon Blanc and Pinot they also produce Riesling and Chardonnay, and their Pinot Gris sells out within two months of release. A Noble Sauvignon Blanc is produced in selected years and this, along with a number of older vintages, is available only at the cellar door. Unusually, Isabel also produces a half-bottle of Sauvignon Blanc, and has a small production of olive oil which also sells out quickly. A pleasant place to bring a picnic and enjoy the views across the grapes to the Richmond Ranges, and for those who want a longer stay among the vines a three-bedroom lodge is available.

Located away from the main grape-growing district, on the road between Blenheim and Picton, Johanneshof's vineyards are unusual for the Marlborough area in that the vineyard has been established on a steep hillside of clay soil — in direct contrast to the free-draining gravels of the Wairau plain. Noted for their award-winning Gewürztraminer and Pinot Gris, Johanneshof also grow Pinot Noir and Sauvignon Blanc. They also produce brandy, grappa, two sparkling wines and dessert wines (though not every vintage).

Established in 1991 by German-born Edel Everling and New Zealander Warwick Foley, the free-spirited nature of Johanneshof is also evident in the playful landscaping of the vineyard (picnic facilities are available), which extends to an extraordinary underground barrel room. Built by West Coast goldminers deep into solid rock, the cave indeed looks every bit the classic gold mine of cowboy movies with rough-hewn walls and timber reinforcing, but this mine contains liquid gold instead of nuggets. Atmospheric with candles and beautiful wrought-iron gates, the cave holds maturing sparkling wine in bottles, ageing brandy in barrels of French oak, and the wine library, all at a constant 12°C. A delicate black mould like a softly spun velvet lines the cave walls, acting as a litmus test of the cave's constant level of humidity and temperature. There is a charge for touring the wine cave and you need to book ahead.

Johanneshof Cellars

State Highway 1, Koromiko (between Picton and Blenheim)

Labels Johanneshof Cellars

Specialisation Gewürztraminer
Pinot Gris
Sauvignon Blanc

Opening hours
Labour Weekend–1 May
 Tues–Sun 10 am–4 pm
Rest of year phone to check

Tasting $3, refundable on
purchase

Phone 03 573 7035

Website www.johanneshof.co.nz

Lawson's Dry Hills

**238 Alabama Road
Blenheim**

Labels Lawson's Dry Hills

Specialisation Sauvignon Blanc
Gewürztraminer

Opening hours
Daily 10 am–5 pm
except Christmas Day, Good
Friday, Anzac Day morning

Tasting Casual visitors no charge,
charge for groups

Phone **03 578 7674**

Website
www.lawsonsdryhills.co.nz

This family-owned vineyard produces a wide range of wines, all from Marlborough-sourced grapes, including Sauvignon Blanc, Gewürztraminer, Pinot Gris, Riesling, Pinot Noir and a late harvest Chardonnay. The cellar door, set in a rustic building among the vines, has a fine view to the dry Wither Hills that give the winery its name. An old rimu timber floor gives the cellar door a warm welcoming feel which betrays its humble origins as a farm shed. Take a peek around the back of the building and you will see that sections of the old corrugated iron shed still remain. Ross Lawson was one of the early pioneers of screwcaps and Lawson's Dry Hills is believed to be the first winery to have produced all their wines with screwcaps. This was a huge risk at that time, but in the end it was a development that swept through the international wine industry in a few short years.

In addition to wine tasting Lawson's offers cheese platters and wine by the glass. Visitors are welcome to bring a picnic and use the sheltered and shady courtyard alongside the winery. If interested in a winery tour you will need to phone ahead. There is a selected range of gifts for sale including merino wool items, some of which are a possum fur mix, as well as wine books.

Mahi, a family-owned winery, produces a range of single-vineyard, single-variety wines with no blending, all produced from Marlborough-sourced grapes. In addition to Sauvignon Blanc the winery makes Gewürztraminer, Chardonnay and Pinot Noir, and the snail logo on its bottles reflects Mahi's emphasis on quality — making good wine takes time. The restaurant is bright and colourful, featuring New Zealand art and food that has a European influence with a focus on fresh local produce. As well as lunch, visitors can drop by for a cup of coffee or a glass of wine, sitting in the sun in summer or by the open fire in winter. If the cellar door staff are not too busy, ask to see their barrel-lined caves set seven metres into the hillside behind the winery.

Mahi Wines

9 Terrace Road
Renwick

Labels **Mahi**

Specialisation **Sauvignon Blanc**

Opening hours
Daily 10 am–4.30 pm
Restaurant
  Lunch from 10.30 am Wed–Sun
  Dinner Friday night

Tasting **No charge**
Phone **03 572 8859**
Website **www.mahiwine.co.nz**

Montana Brancott Winery

Main South Road (SH 1) Blenheim

Labels Brancott
        Montana
        Stoneleigh

Specialisation Sauvignon Blanc
                Pinot Noir
                Deutz Marlborough
                Cuvée

Opening hours
Daily 10 am–4.30 pm
Restaurant 10.30 am–3 pm

Tasting Free tasting of four wines
         (choose from at least 16),
         charge for tasting trays of
         premium wines

Phone 03 577 5775

Website
www.brancottvineyards.com

Montana is the largest winery in New Zealand and in 1976 was the first winery to set up in Marlborough, much to the surprise of many who dismissed all of the South Island as too cold for grape growing. The name Brancott refers to its vineyards in the Brancott Valley. Montana's vineyards are spread throughout New Zealand and produce a dazzling array of wines that vary in both type and range, though the wines available for tasting and sale here at Blenheim are all Reserve quality and up. In addition to wine for sale and tasting, Montana at Brancott has a wide selection of gift items for sale — all New Zealand products — ranging from wine-related items to local produce and a select range of giftware. For those wishing to extend their nose for wines, there is an aroma wheel for testing sense of smell which is both fun and educational.

Brancott is in fact Montana's main winery for the company, and it is one of the few wineries to offer tours of its extensive plant (these are on the hour from 10 am to 3 pm). For those wanting more, Montana also offers a half-day 'Odyssey' tour which includes the vineyard, winery, wine tasting and a wine-matched lunch (bookings essential).

Loosely inspired by French chateau style, the scale of the main winery retains a welcoming aspect with high ceilings, woodwork, rustic flooring and large open fireplaces. The spacious restaurant spills out onto a sunny terrace in the summer, while in winter a snug fire provides both warmth and a cheery welcome on the chilliest of days. Relaxed and catering for almost every taste, the family café is reasonably priced, has a children's menu (there is an outdoor playground as well), and has light meals in addition to a lunch menu. Or you can just have a break with a coffee or a glass of wine.

If you are really tight on time, this winery on the main highway is the most accessible of Marlborough's wineries and well set up for visitors.

Nautilus Estate

**12 Rapaura Road
Renwick**

Labels   Nautilus
             Twin Islands

Specialisation   Pinot Noir

Opening hours
Daily 10.30 am–4.30 pm except
    Christmas Day, Good Friday

Tasting   No charge
Phone   03 572 9364
Website   www.nautilusestate.com

In a wine region dominated by Sauvignon Blanc, at Nautilus Pinot Noir dominates. So much so that the winery is purpose-built to handle this one grape variety. Pinot Noir is difficult to grow, and the less damage to the fruit during the post-harvest processing the better the wine. The Nautilus winery, the first of its kind in the southern hemisphere, is designed to be as gentle as possible on grapes, including being gravity-fed to ensure the least possible damage. The compact winery offers ad hoc tours depending on how busy they are, but groups need to phone ahead. However, a large viewing window allows visitors a good look into the barrel hall and winery. Within the tasting room there is an aroma station to challenge your taste buds with a litmus paper test to check results.

In addition to Pinot Noir, family-owned Nautilus also produces Pinot Gris, Chardonnay, Sauvignon Blanc and a sparkling cuvée. Cheese platters are available, or bring a picnic. Also for sale is local olive oil, Zerutti glassware, wine books and, of course, nautilus shells.

Saint Clair Estate Wines

Cnr Rapaura and Selmes Roads Blenheim

Labels Saint Clair

Specialisation Sauvignon Blanc
Pinot Noir

Opening hours
Daily 9 am–5 pm
except Christmas and Boxing Days, Good Friday, Anzac Day morning

Tasting **No charge**

Phone **03 570 5280**

Website **www.stclair.co.nz**

Wrapped around by vines on three sides, this friendly winery has an international reputation for its Sauvignon Blanc and fine range of Reserve wines including Gewürztraminer, Riesling, Merlot, Pinot Gris, Chardonnay, Pinot Noir and Noble Riesling. It is one of the early vineyards in Marlborough, established in 1978 by Neal and Judy Ibbotson, and is still top of the class, winning the trophy for Best New Zealand Wine Producer of the Year in 2005 at the International Wine and Spirit Competition. The tasting room and café are wide open to the sun, and the food style and service are very relaxed: you can have just a cup of coffee and cake, something more substantial, or take time out with a glass of wine soaking up the rays. There is a pétanque court, plenty of space for the kids to run around and, in addition to the food and wine, Saint Clair have for sale a selected range of wine glassware.

Sharing the same car park and right next door is Traditional Country Preserves, which offers tastings of its huge range of preserves, jams, chutneys, sauces and pickles — all home-made on the premises.
(www.traditionalcountrypreserves.co.nz)

Established by New Zealand-born and UK-based film-maker Michael Seresin, this vineyard has quickly established a reputation for high-quality wines from its three organic and biodynamic vineyards in Marlborough. While best known for Pinot Noir and Sauvignon Blanc, Seresin also produces excellent Chardonnay, Gewürztraminer, Riesling, Pinot Gris and an innovative and unusual oaked Sauvignon Blanc. Quality is paramount and all the fruit is hand-picked.

The unpretentious tasting room is relaxed and friendly. It is tucked in behind the busy winery where it is possible to see what is going on at different times of the year. The winery sits on a small rise above the plain, giving the visitor an excellent view over the surrounding vineyards and across to the Richmond Ranges.

Seresin has substantial olive plantations with olive trees lining the drive to the winery, and Tuscan olive oil expert Maurizio Castelli visits New Zealand to oversee the harvesting and pressing. All organic and in a wide range of flavours, Seresin's olive oil is available for tasting. Also on offer is local honey and seasonal jams.

Seresin Estate

Bedford Road
Blenheim

Labels **Seresin**

Specialisation **Pinot Noir**
Sauvignon Blanc

Opening hours
Daily 10 am–4.30 pm

Tasting **No charge**
Phone **03 572 9408**
Website **www.seresin.co.nz**

Spy Valley Wines

Lake Timara Road
Off Waihopai Valley Road
Renwick

Labels Spy Valley
Envoy

Specialisation Sauvignon Blanc
Riesling
Pinot Gris

Opening hours
Labour Weekend–Anzac Day
daily 10 am–4 pm
Rest of year
Mon–Fri 10 am–4 pm

Tasting Casual visitors no charge,
small charge for groups
of 10+

Phone **03 572 9840**

Website **www.spyvalleywine.co.nz**

Taking its name from the nearby satellite monitoring site, this family-owned vineyard is known for its cool-climate grape varieties, and in addition to its respected Sauvignon Blanc it also produces Riesling, Pinot Gris, Merlot, Pinot Noir and in a good year a Noble Riesling. Opened in 2003, this smart modern winery features an award-winning tasting room designed by New Zealand architects Wraight and Associates, contemporary New Zealand art by Tom Sladden, wine antiques and a dramatic outdoor sculpture which picks up on the spy theme. The entrance to the tasting room is via an innovative water garden which uses stylish grasses and aquatic plants. Continuing on the espionage trail, Spy Valley is also famous for its innovative tee shirts with text such as 'Caught red handed in the Valley of the Spies'. In addition to wine, Spy Valley also produces its own olive oil. While on the fringe of the winery area, Spy Valley is well worth the drive.

Producing single-vineyard wines from select Marlborough vineyards, Te Whare Ra has created a surprising range of wines including Pinot Noir, Syrah, Sauvignon Blanc, Gewürztraminer, Pinot Gris, Riesling, Chardonnay and Toru, an appealing wine unusually blended from Gewürztraminer, Pinot Gris and Riesling. Family-owned and established in 1979, Te Whare Ra is the oldest boutique vineyard in the Marlborough region and some of the original plantings are nearly 30 years old. The current owners, husband and wife team Anna and Jason Flowerday, both are winemakers with a long professional and family association with the wine industry. Anna was a national finalist in the Wine Society Young Australian Winemaker of the Year 2002.

Their Gewürztraminers, made in small quantities, are among the best in the country and sell out quickly, but there is a very good chance that some will be available at the cellar door. All the wines are processed on site and both Anna and Jason serve visitors at their cosy upstairs cellar door overlooking the vineyard and beyond to the Richmond Ranges. The cellar door is not always attended, so just ring the bell.

Te Whare Ra Wines

56 Anglesea Street Renwick

Labels Te Whare Ra

Specialisation Gewürztraminer
Riesling
Syrah

Opening hours
Labour Weekend–Easter
 Daily 11 am–4.30 pm
Rest of year
 Thurs–Sun

Tasting No charge

Phone 03 572 8581

Website www.te-whare-ra.co.nz

Jaap van der Stoel

The Wine Room

State Highway 1
Blenheim

Labels   Kim Crawford
          Tohu
          St Lukes
          Omaka Springs
          Summerhouse

Specialisation   Showcasing wines
                  from five wineries

Opening hours
Daily 10 am–4.30 pm

Tasting   Five wines $10,
           selection white wines $12,
           selection red wines $15
Phone   03 570 5490
Website
www.thewineroom.net.nz

This newly established venture on State Highway 1 just north of Blenheim is the showroom for five wineries, not all of them from Marlborough: Tohu (Gisborne), Kim Crawford (Hawke's Bay) and St Lukes, Omaka Springs and Summerhouse (Marlborough). This is an excellent opportunity to taste not only wine from around the country, but also that from several smaller vineyards without their own cellar door. In addition, it is possible to do comparative tasting across several regions and vintages. Annie's Café is adjacent and there is an enclosed children's playground as well.

Surrounded by Sauvignon Blanc vines, Wairau River's restaurant and tasting room is a stylish building inspired by the high-country homestead, with wide verandas hung with wisteria, and constructed of mudbrick blocks weighing a hefty 85 kg each and made on site. Matching the dun-coloured brick, massive rimu beams from the old Wairau hospital and a stone fireplace create the homely atmosphere, snug and warm in the winter while cool and shady in the summer. The restaurant is bistro-style with an emphasis on fresh seasonal foods, and for a winery eatery is reasonably priced. It also has a children's menu (there is plenty of space for kids to run around outside), or you can just drop by for coffee and cake or a quiet glass of wine by the fire. This restaurant was one of four finalists in the 2006 Winery Restaurant Awards.

Established in 1978 on land bordering the Wairau River, this is one of the oldest family-owned vineyards in Marlborough and has two ranges under its single label: the Estate range of blended wines and Home Block, the single-vineyard range. All the grapes come from Wairau River vineyards in Marlborough and include Sauvignon Blanc, Pinot Gris, Gewürztraminer, Pinot Noir, Chardonnay and Riesling; some of the wines are exclusive to the cellar door.

Wairau River Wines

Cnr State Highway 6 and Rapaura Road Renwick

Labels Wairau River

Specialisation Sauvignon Blanc
Pinot Gris
Gewürztraminer

Opening hours
Daily 10 am–5 pm
Lunch 12 noon–3 pm
Closed Christmas Day, Good
Friday

Tasting Casual visitors no charge,
charge for larger groups

Phone 03 572 7950

Website
www.wairauriverwines.com

Wither Hills Vineyard

211 New Renwick Road Blenheim

Labels Wither Hills

Specialisation Sauvignon Blanc
Pinot Noir
Chardonnay

Opening hours
Daily 10 am–4.30 pm

Tasting **No charge**
Phone **03 520 8270**
Website **www.witherhills.co.nz**

Without a doubt one of this country's most stylish vineyards, Wither Hills is worth visiting for its architecture as well as its wines. Combining the functionality of a working vineyard with a form that blends into the distinct Marlborough environment, the building and landscaping strongly reflect both the topography and the colours of the region. Unusually for a winery of this size, Wither Hills produces just three types of wine, though it has occasionally produced a Noble Riesling depending on the vintage — available only at the cellar door. While best known for its Sauvignon Blanc, the Wither Hills Pinot Noir is also a consistent award-winner.

The entrance to the building is up wide steps flanked by deep tussock leading to a modern, open tasting room. From the top of the winery there is a fine view over the Wairau Valley, while dug underground is an atmospheric barrel hall that is well worth the visit. The stone for the building comes from the hills above their vineyard at Rarangi. There is a specially constructed gantry behind the tasting room which allows visitors to have an excellent view over the working winery. The winery is very popular for private functions and can also arrange personalised tastings for groups in a separate area.

This pleasant family-owned vineyard has a small tasting room raised above the eight-hectare vineyard overlooking Pinot Noir and Merlot grapes, with a long view over the vines to the Moutere Hills, Kahurangi Mountains and Abel Tasman National Park. All the grapes for Brightwater's wines are sourced within a kilometre of the winery, and include Sauvignon Blanc, Riesling, Merlot, Pinot Noir, Noble Sauvignon Blanc and an ice wine. Their 2006 Riesling was named as one of the top 10 New Zealand Rieslings and won two golds in the Liquorland Top 100 Wine Competition.

The cellar door is usually staffed by either the owners Gary and Valley Neale or the winemaker — all are naturally enthusiastic about winemaking and are happy to show visitors around the winery if time permits. At the cellar door is a collection of menus from local restaurants so you can even sort out where and what to eat, and buy wine to match. How's that for helpful? The cellar door also has local Nelson art for sale.

Brightwater Vineyard

546 Main Road
Hope, Nelson

Labels **Brightwater**

Specialisation **Sauvignon Blanc Riesling**

Opening hours
Labour Weekend–Easter daily 11 am–5 pm

Tasting **No charge**

Phone **03 544 1066**

Website
www.brightwaterwine.co.nz

Fossil Ridge

Hart Road
Richmond, Nelson

Labels Fossil Ridge

Specialisation Chardonnay
Riesling

Opening hours
Nov–Easter daily 11 am–5 pm

Tasting $5 for four wines, olives
and macadamia nuts

Phone 03 544 7459

Website www.fossilridge.co.nz

This family-owned boutique vineyard is one of the closest wineries to Nelson city, and at just three hectares it is also one of the smallest. All its wines are produced from this single vineyard. The winery takes its name from the rare marine fossils of *Monotis richmondiana* (the winery has fossils on display) which are unique to just two places in the world, one of which is this vineyard. In addition to Chardonnay and Riesling, Fossil Ridge also produces Pinot Noir, Gewürztraminer and Rosé, with all its grapes hand-picked and bunch-pressed.

Bare land just 10 years ago, Fossil Ridge is now an oasis of duck ponds, vines, trees and garden with ducks and pukeko fossicking among the vines and the waterlily-covered pond. The intimate cellar door, with its beautifully polished eucalypt floors, has a terrace overlooking the ponds and visitors are encouraged to walk through vines and the olive grove. From this grove Fossil Ridge makes its own olive oil and pickled olives, as well as producing macadamia nuts and making lime marmalade from the kaffir limes grown on the estate. Local art is also for sale. Tasting trays of four wines along with olives and macadamia nuts can be enjoyed out on the terrace by the pond.

Greenhough Vineyard and Winery

A long-established vineyard, Greenhough has some of the oldest vines in the Nelson region, with its earliest vines planted in 1976 at Hope. Sourcing grapes from three vineyards in the Nelson area in addition to the five-hectare Hope vineyard, Greenhough has two distinct ranges under its one label. The White Label is for wines from the Hope vineyard, and here Pinot Noir dominates. Under the Yellow Label are wines from the other vineyards, including Gewürztraminer, Pinot Noir, Pinot Blanc, Sauvignon Blanc, Riesling and Chardonnay. However, some are produced only in small quantities, and the White Label and Pinot Blanc are available only at the cellar door.

Family-owned, the cellar door is usually operated by one of the owners and is set in a light and open plastered building overlooking grape vines and olive trees.

Paton's Road
Hope, Nelson

Labels **Greenhough**

Specialisation **Pinot Noir**
Gewürztraminer
Sauvignon Blanc
Riesling

Opening hours
Labour Weekend–Boxing Day
  Sat/Sun 1 pm–5 pm
Boxing Day–end Jan
  daily 1 pm–5 pm

Tasting   No charge, groups by
         appointment
Phone   **03 542 3868**
Email   greenhough.vineyard@
        clear.net.nz

Aromatics

Aromatics are white wines that have a pronounced aroma, particularly grapey, floral or spicy, e.g. Riesling, Pinot Gris, Gewürztraminer.

Kaimira Estate Winery

121 River Terrace Road
Brightwater, Nelson

Labels **Kaimira**

Specialisation **Riesling**
Sauvignon Blanc
Chardonnay

Opening hours
Labour Weekend–Easter
daily 11 am–5 pm

Tasting **No charge**

Phone **03 542 3491**

Website **www.kaimirawines.com**

Within the Kaimira label there are two ranges: Brightwater for wines produced from hand-picked grapes from the home vineyard only, and Nelson for wines from regionally sourced grapes. Known for good value for money, this family-owned vineyard produces a wide range of wines including Syrah, an Alsace-style Gewürztraminer, Viognier, Pinot Noir, Riesling, Pinot Gris, Sauvignon Blanc and Chardonnay. The new tasting room, built in 2007, is located on the banks of the Wairoa River on very stony soil and features works by local Nelson artists.

Neudorf
Vineyards

Neudorf Road
Upper Moutere, Nelson

Labels **Neudorf**

Specialisation **Pinot Noir**
Chardonnay

Opening hours
Most of year daily
 10 am–5 pm
'In the depths of winter'
 Sat/Sun only

Tasting No charge but a donation
 to Child Cancer Research
 is appreciated

Phone **03 543 2643**

Website **www.neudorf.co.nz**

Established in 1978 by Tim and Judy Finn, who still own the winery, the name Neudorf (after the road the winery is located on) reflects the nineteenth-century settlement of the area by German immigrants. Neudorf takes pride in creating elegant, fine wines that age well, particularly Chardonnay but also Sauvignon Blanc, Riesling, Pinot Gris, Pinot Noir and Rosé.

What makes a visit to Neudorf special is a wonderful mixture of new and old buildings which artfully combine the rustic with the modern. There is no pretence that this is anything other than a working winery, but the 140-year-old barn with slightly peeling paint and mosses blends naturally with other farm-style buildings just a few years old. The garden setting is superb and careful attention to detail makes this one of New Zealand's most attractive wineries. A broad wooden veranda faces out over a lovely lawn set with tables, overlooking the vines and shaded by an ancient maple tree (*Acer negundo*). Accessed by a beautiful tree-lined drive, the lawn hosts occasional concerts and the tables are quickly occupied in the summer months. While Neudorf does not provide food, the local Moutere area is well known for its excellent local fare — so the idea is to spend some time gathering up local goodies and then head off to Neudorf for a picnic with excellent wines.

Ruby Bay Lodge and Vineyard

271 Pomona Road
Ruby Bay, Nelson

Labels **Ruby Bay**

Specialisation **Sauvignon Blanc**
Pinot Noir

Opening hours
Labour Weekend–Easter
  Thurs–Mon 11 am–4 pm
Rest of year
  Sat/Sun 11 am–4 pm (call ahead)

Tasting **No charge**

Phone **03 540 3938**

Website
www.rubybayvineyard.co.nz

Located in rolling hill country just behind Ruby Bay, the cellar door sits high on a ridge looking out over the vineyard and beyond that to a great view out over Tasman Bay and far to the east. Established by Sam and Audrey Watt in 2002 on the site of an apple orchard, the five hectares on clay soils now produce five wines: Sauvignon Blanc, Pinot Noir, Chardonnay, Riesling and Pinot Gris. The small scale of the vineyard means that visitors to the attractive cellar door are more than likely to enjoy tasting Ruby Bay wines with the friendly owners, and their wines are available only at the cellar door or by mail order.

In addition to wine tasting and sales, Ruby Bay also has on offer chocolate truffles made especially for the vineyard and featuring its wines as tasty centres. There is also accommodation in two lodge suites and a self-contained cottage (see the website for details).

Established in 1973 by Austrian-born Hermann Seifried and his New Zealand wife Agnes, Seifried Estate was one of the earliest vineyards in the Nelson region. Now with 155 hectares in grapes Seifried produces a surprising range of wines that reflect the preference in the Nelson region for white aromatics and the European influence of Hermann. All the wines are from Nelson-sourced grapes, and this vineyard was the first in the Nelson area to be certified sustainable. Producing Gewürztraminer, Sauvignon Blanc, Cabernet Sauvignon, Cabernet Merlot, Riesling, Pinot Gris, Pinot Noir, ice wine, barrique-fermented Chardonnay, and in the right years late harvest wines, Seifried is the only winery in the country to produce Würzer, a sweet white wine, and Sylvia, a red wine made from Zweigelt grapes. These last two wines are available only in the Nelson region and at the cellar door, which also has older vintages for sale.

The large country-style restaurant has a relaxed atmosphere and features Nelson produce, and is particularly strong on fresh seafood from Tasman Bay. Family-focused with a children's playground, Seifried's is open for lunch or just a coffee or glass of wine in the pleasant outdoor courtyard. The cellar door has wine-related gifts for sale, locally made chocolate truffles and grape juice. Seifried also has gift-wrapped bottles of wine, which helpfully cuts out one more job if you are giving wine as a gift.

Seifried Estate

Cnr State Highway 60 and Redwood Road (Rabbit Island turnoff) Appleby, Nelson

Labels **Seifried**
          Old Coach Road

Specialisation **Gewürztraminer**
                 Sauvignon Blanc
                 Riesling
                 Pinot Gris

Opening hours
Daily 10 am–5 pm

Tasting **$3, refundable on purchase**

Phone **03 544 1555**

Website **www.seifried.co.nz**

Te Mania & Richmond Plains Wines

**Grape Escape
McShane Road
Richmond, Nelson**

Labels Te Mania
        Richmond Plains

Specialisation Pinot Noir
                Chardonnay
                Sauvignon Blanc
                Blanc de Noir

Opening hours
Daily 10.30 am–4.30 pm

Tasting 50c per wine plus a free
         tasting of the Wine of the
         Month

Phone 03 544 4341

Websites

www.temaniawines.co.nz

www.richmondplains.co.nz

These two distinct labels are now part of one company, and operate a tasting room in a small retail complex called the Grape Escape on the busy highway to Moutere. Richmond Plains is certified organic and produces Rosé, Sauvignon Blanc, Chardonnay, Pinot Noir (plus a Reserve Pinot Noir) and the Admiral, an easy-drinking blended red. In addition it produces Blanc de Noir, made from Pinot Noir grapes as a white wine, which sells out fast. Te Mania also has a broad range of wines including Pinot Noir Rosé, Riesling, Sauvignon Blanc, Pinot Gris, Chardonnay, Pinot Noir Syrah and, in the right years, a Botrytis Riesling. Te Mania took a gold medal at the Air New Zealand Wine Awards for its Pinot Noir, unusual in that the Nelson region is better known for its aromatic whites.

At the Grape Escape the tasting room is tucked towards the back of the group of interconnected retail outlets alongside a café that offers platters along with a wide range of café food. Also in the shops are Prenzels products, paintings, candles and pottery, while outside are a children's playground and llamas and other exotic animals.

Waimea
Estates Winery

**Appleby Highway
Hope, Nelson**

Labels **Waimea
Spinyback**

Specialisation **Sauvignon Blanc
Pinot Noir
Gewürztraminer**

Opening hours
**Labour Weekend–Easter
daily 11 am–5 pm
Rest of year
Wed–Sun 11 am–4 pm**

Tasting **50c per tasting, refundable
on purchase**

Phone **03 544 6385**

Website
www.waimeaestates.co.nz

A popular local winery, Waimea Estate combines cellar door and wine sales with one of the most pleasant vineyard cafés in the Nelson region. Established in 1993, Waimea produced its first vintage in 1997 and has a strong emphasis on the white aromatics for which the Nelson area is rapidly gaining a strong reputation. The two labels are quite distinct, with the Spinyback range fruit-driven, easy-drinking and more affordable. The Waimea range includes Sauvignon Blanc, Pinot Noir, Gewürztraminer, Pinot Gris, Riesling, Chardonnay, Noble Riesling, Cabernet Sauvignon/Merlot and Viognier, with the Waimea Gewürztraminer winning the trophy at the 2006 Royal Easter Show. Under the Waimea label the winery also has the Bolitho range, produced in small quantities from signature vineyards and sold only through restaurants and the cellar door. In addition back vintages are available through the restaurant.

Set among the vines, this popular and reasonably priced restaurant is open for lunch, featuring a country cuisine based on fresh local produce for which Nelson, with its equitable sunny climate, is famous. Overlooking Sauvignon Blanc vines, there is spacious indoor and outdoor seating, live music every Sunday and a revolving art exhibition that changes every six weeks.

Waimea works with local iwi Ngati Koata in raising funds for tuatara protection (hence the name Spinyback) – 5 cents from every Spinyback bottle sold goes to help tuatara.

Daniel Schuster

Reeces Road
Off State Highway 1
2 km north of Waipara

Labels **Daniel Schuster**

Specialisation **Pinot Noir**
Sauvignon Blanc
Chardonnay
Riesling

Opening hours
Daily 10 am–5.30 pm

Tasting **$3 for six wines,**
refundable on purchase

Phone **03 314 5901**

Website
www.danielschusterwines.co.nz

One of New Zealand's iconic winemakers, Daniel Schuster has been closely associated with the rise of the wine industry since the late 1970s. He established this vineyard in 1986, and the Pinot Noir grapes in front of the winery are over 20 years old. The wines are all made from Waipara and Canterbury grapes, and the range includes Pinot Noir, Chardonnay, Riesling, Sauvignon Blanc and a late harvest Riesling.

The winery is elegant and modern, built low to take advantage of the expansive views over the North Canterbury countryside. Designed by architect David McBride, who also designed the equally smart Mt Difficulty in Central Otago, the tasting room has beautiful tiled floors and a wide terrace to catch the sun, complete with stylish sundial that actually works. The cellar door offers coffee, selected gifts, olive oil and cellar tours by arrangement, and there is every chance that you will meet Daniel Schuster himself.

Malolactic fermentation

This is a secondary fermentation and a process of change in the wine, where tart malic acid (the acid in apples) is converted into softer-tasting lactic acid (the acid in milk and yoghurt). Malolactic conversion can be initiated or prevented as required by the winemaker. Wines that have undergone this process are generally rounder with a fuller mouth-feel, richer and more buttery.

Perched on a limestone bluff overlooking South Bay with views of mountains and sea, this must be one of New Zealand's most spectacularly sited vineyards – where else in the world can you whale-watch and wine-taste at the same time? Humpback whales come right into the shallow waters on occasion, and dolphins are frequently seen in the bay below. Inland the brutally rugged Kaikoura Ranges rise sharply, shimmering blue in the summer and topped with snow in the winter.

The wines are made from grapes grown in Kaikoura and Marlborough, and include Sauvignon Blanc, Pinot Noir, Pinot Gris, Gewürztraminer, late harvest Riesling, Chardonnay and Rosé. However, the vintages from the exposed Kaikoura site of clay over limestone are much more variable. For something very different, try the Kaikoura Cream, a wine-based cream liqueur.

Kaikoura has an intriguing underground barrel hall, and tours are available on the hour from 10 am to 4 pm. Over 30 metres long, and buried deep into the hillside, the cellar is a consistent 12°C all year round. The tours, which take around 30 minutes, cover local history, wine types, wine equipment and wine processes, and finish with wine tasting underground.

Visitors are welcome to bring a picnic, though the winery has available a deli-bar fridge for vineyard platters and cheese tasting, the famous 'Kaikoura Toastie' sandwich, soup, ice cream, beer, coffee and tea. There are both outdoor seating and indoor tables with picture windows overlooking the sea. A small gift shop offers a wide range of mainly locally made gifts including pottery, possum skin hats and beautifully carved walking and tramping sticks. Local olive oil tastings are available on request.

Kaikoura's barrel hall is the setting for the local 'Trash Fashion' competition where clothing is made from discarded rubbish. Kaikoura also holds a 48-hour photography competition in June and an 'Art In the Dark' display in March in the barrel hall (see the website for details).

Kaikoura Winery

State Highway 1
2 km south of Kaikoura

Labels **Kaikoura**

Specialisation **Sauvignon Blanc
Gewürztraminer
Pinot Noir**

Opening hours
**Daily 10 am–5.30 pm
except Christmas Day, Good
Friday, Anzac Day morning**

Tasting **$4 for full range of wines**

Phone **03 319 7966**

Website
www.kaikourawinery.co.nz

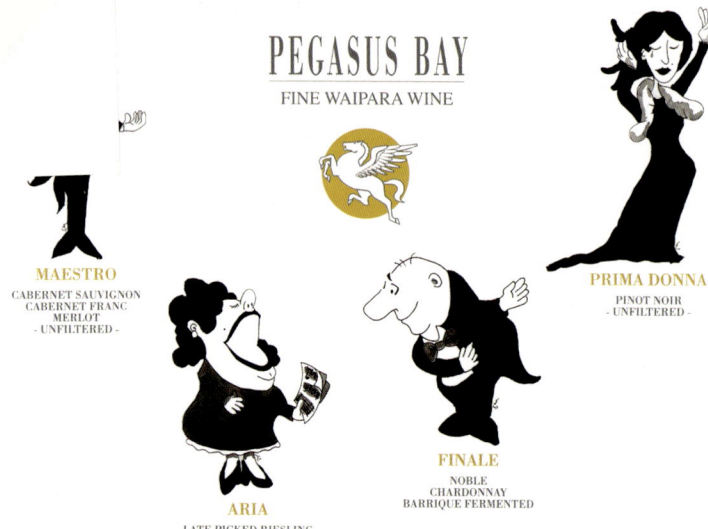

PEGASUS BAY

FINE WAIPARA WINE

MAESTRO
CABERNET SAUVIGNON
CABERNET FRANC
MERLOT
- UNFILTERED -

PRIMA DONNA
PINOT NOIR
- UNFILTERED -

FINALE
NOBLE
CHARDONNAY
BARRIQUE FERMENTED

ARIA
- LATE PICKED RIESLING -

Pegasus Bay Winery

263 Stockgrove Road
Off State Highway 1
1 km south of Waipara

Labels Pegasus Bay
        Main Divide

Specialisation Pinot Noir
               Riesling

Opening hours
Daily 10.30 am–5 pm
Restaurant 12 noon–4 pm

Tasting $2 per tasting, refundable
          on purchase or when
          dining

Phone   03 314 6869

Websites **www.pegasusbay.com**
          www.maindivide.com

Although the first vintage was produced only in 1991, it was Pegasus Bay's wines — and its Pinot Noir in particular — that drew attention to the Waipara Valley, with its hot dry summers and free-draining gravelly soils, as a premium wine-growing area. The Pegasus Bay range is made from estate-grown Waipara grapes and is their premium range while the Main Divide range is produced from contract-grown South Island fruit. The winery is still owned by the Donaldson family who established the original vineyard. The cellar door often has older vintages available that are not easily sourced elsewhere. From the spacious tasting room, a large plate window gives a peek into the barrel hall and wine library.

The restaurant has an equally impressive reputation and overlooks gardens with a wide view to the north. Open for lunch, its food style is influenced by contemporary European cuisine, though based on fresh local ingredients. This is a popular restaurant and bookings are essential especially for groups, although there is also the opportunity to just have a glass or two of wine with cheese, or coffee. The winery hosts summer concerts in a natural amphitheatre and opera evenings through winter (see the website for details).

Torlesse Wines exudes a rustic charm with its rich red corrugated-iron building, an old insulated railway carriage that serves as a barrel room, and a friendly welcome at the cellar door. Producing a surprising range of wines, Torlesse sources its grapes from a variety of terrain in the Waipara area, from valley floor to steep terraced hillsides. The winery has two ranges: Torlesse are introductory style wines which include Sauvignon Blanc, Riesling, Gewürztraminer, Chardonnay, Sticky Riesling, Rosé and Cabernet/Merlot; and Omihi Road are Reserve wines covering Pinot Noir, Riesling, Sauvignon Blanc, Pinot Gris, Gewürztraminer, Merlot and Chardonnay. Also produced, though in smaller quantities and often available only at the cellar door, are Tawny Port and Cassis, a rich fortified wine made from blackcurrants. The grape variety for the port varies from year to year.

The knowledgeable cellar door staff are more than likely to be either the owners or the winemaker, so this is good chance to expand your wine knowledge while tasting the wines. Local art and produce, including olive oil, are also for sale at the cellar door.

Torlesse Wines

State Highway 1
Waipara

Labels **Torlesse**
       Omihi Road

Specialisation **Pinot Gris**
             Riesling

Opening hours
Fri–Sun daily 11 am–5 pm

Tasting **Casual visitors no charge,
small charge for groups**

Phone **03 314 6929**

Website **www.torlesse.co.nz**

Waipara Springs Winery

State Highway 1
Waipara

Labels **Waipara Springs**

Specialisation **Pinot Noir**
Riesling

Opening hours
Daily 11 am–5 pm

Tasting **$3 per tasting**
Phone **03 314 6777**

Website
www.waiparasprings.co.nz

One of the first boutique vineyards in the Waipara district, this winery initially started out with Chardonnay but in recent years it has been the area's signature wine, Pinot Noir, for which Waipara Springs has been recognised. Their 2003 Reserve Pinot Noir won gold in both the Air New Zealand Wine Awards and the Sydney Wine Competition. Waipara Springs Reserve wines are bottled under the Premo range and include Pinot Noir, Chardonnay, Sauvignon Blanc and Riesling, while the more everyday wines under the Waipara Springs range cover Sauvignon Blanc, Riesling, Chardonnay, Cabernet Sauvignon/Merlot and a Blush.

The café is a firm favourite with day visitors from Christchurch, and for very good reason. The food is freshly made on the premises, reasonably priced and varied, from coffee and cake through to platters and more substantial lunch dishes. During the winter a fire ensures that patrons are kept warm and cosy, while in summer the casual atmosphere in the large garden draws the crowds (booking is essential at weekends). There is local art for sale and occasionally the winery hosts live music.

Claiming the honour of being New Zealand's highest-altitude vineyard at 440 metres above sea level, Clay Cliffs lies on the outskirts of Omarama, better known for its high-altitude gliding than for its wine. From the Clay Cliffs label, which is estate-grown, comes Pinot Gris, Muscat, Pinot Blanc and Pinot Noir, while the Mt Cook label is reserved for grapes brought in from other growers and includes Sauvignon Blanc, Riesling and Chardonnay. The wine is made by Dean Shaw at the Central Otago Wine Company.

The simple Sante Fe-inspired restaurant has a style very suited to the dry Mackenzie landscape and is complemented by attractive gardens with shade trees and ponds and a play area for the kids. Open for both lunch and dinner, the restaurant has an international flavour with fresh New Zealand ingredients at its heart.

Clay Cliffs Estate

1 Pinot Noir Court Omarama

Labels **Clay Cliffs**
      Mt Cook

Specialisation **Pinot Gris**

Tasting **$5, refundable on purchase**
Phone **03 438 9654**
Website **www.claycliffs.co.nz**

Tax on wine

Wine is highly taxed in New Zealand. In addition to GST there are currently two taxes on wine with an alcoholic content under 15%: excise tax at $2.332 per litre and Alcohol Advisory Council (ALAC) tax at $0.052 per litre. Ports, sherries and other wines over 15% are taxed at an even higher rate.

French Farm Winery

12 Winery Road,
off French Farm
Valley Road,
near Akaroa

Labels French Farm

Specialisation Pinot Noir
Sauvignon Blanc

Opening hours
Daily 10 am–4 pm

Tasting $1 per tasting
Phone 03 304 5784
Website www.frenchfarm.co.nz

A French-provincial-style winery overlooking the sea, French Farm produces a small range of single-vineyard wines all grown on-site, and include Pinot Noir, Sauvignon Blanc, Riesling and Chardonnay, with Pinot Gris and Rosé planned for the near future. French Farm wines are available only directly from the winery.

The building was designed by architect Neil Armstrong, and features both formal and casual dining, indoors with an open fireplace and outside in a sheltered courtyard. Open for lunch only, the food style tends towards comfort food and seasonal produce, with a strong emphasis on the fresh. The prices are reasonable with locally farmed Akaroa salmon a firm favourite, as are the fresh salads and home-made desserts. There is a children's menu to satisfy the younger ones (with plenty of space outside for kids to run around) and an outdoor pizzeria; alternatively there is a picnic area in the rose gardens complete with a pétanque court.

French Farm was known to early French settlers as Duke Decazes Bay and was from 1843 to 1847 the site of a French naval station farm. The name eventually was contracted to French Farm.

Langdale is a distinctive corrugated-iron-clad winery restaurant set among the vineyard and large sheltered gardens in West Melton. Access is down a drive lined with tall Lombardy poplars, and from the car park a footbridge crosses over a fast-flowing stream of crystal-clear water. Tastings are available, not only for Langdale wines, but also for other small local producers. On Sundays winemakers from several of these boutique wineries, including Bay Glen, Rattletrack and Braided River, offer tastings of their wines at Langdale between 11 am and 4 pm (tasting charges apply). Wine is also available by the glass.

Along with wine, Langdale has for sale a mouth-watering range of locally made pickles, jams, jellies, chutneys, vinegars and vinaigrettes, olive oils, walnut oil and other produce. With an emphasis on taste and with a hint of the Mediterranean, the spacious open café, surrounded by wide lawns, prides itself on serving fresh seasonal produce and uses free-range eggs and organic flour and bacon. The range of home-baked cakes and breads is fabulous, so it is worth the drive just for coffee and cake. Bookings are recommended on the weekends. The walls are hung with local art for sale, and on or about 1 April the winery hosts Fool's Day Festival.

Langdale Vineyard Restaurant

**161 Langdales Road
West Melton
(near Christchurch)**

Labels Langdale

Specialisation Pinot Noir
Pinot Gris
Riesling

Opening hours
Summer Wed–Sun
11 am–4 pm
Winter Thurs–Sun
11 am–4 pm

Tasting $6, refundable on
purchase

Phone 03 342 6266

Website
www.langdalerestaurant.com

Opihi Vineyard

804 Opihi Road
Hanging Rock
(off SH 8 from Pleasant
Point) near Timaru

Labels **Opihi**

Specialisation **Pinot Gris**

Opening hours
Sept–May Tues–Sun 11 am–4 pm

Tasting **$7 for three wines**
Phone **03 614 8308**
Website **www.opihi.co.nz**

Situated a short distance away on farmland owned by the winery is one of the most spectacular and best known examples of Maori rock art. Easily accessible either on foot or by vehicle, a huge stylised taniwha adorns a limestone overhang and will be easily recognised as it was featured on a New Zealand postage stamp in the 1960s.

Located at the enigmatically named Hanging Rock on the slopes above the Opihi River just inland from Timaru, this vineyard is well worth the short diversion for those travelling along either State Highway 1 between Christchurch and Dunedin or the road to Mount Cook via Geraldine. The free-draining limestone country is particularly suited to Pinot Gris, which is Opihi's flagship wine, but they also produce Pinot Noir, an unusual blend of Müller-Thurgau and Riesling, Chardonnay (both oaked and unoaked) and a late harvest Riesling. Opihi wines are available only from the cellar door or selected outlets in Timaru and Geraldine.

The setting for the café and tasting room is nothing short of ideal. Originally one of the 'down country' homes of high-country-runholder Edward Dark, the beautiful restored homestead was built in 1882 of hand-hewn limestone blocks, quarried just 500 metres from the house. With its warm timber floors it is now a superb café with all mains under $20 at the time of writing! Surrounding the homestead is a broad sweep of lawn, large enough to accommodate a game of cricket or touch rugby, and certainly large enough to accommodate energetic children while their parents contentedly eat and drink on the terrace.

Hanging Rock takes its name from a large rock that perched above the river just below the vineyard. It was for a long time very popular with local youngsters who enjoyed jumping off the rock into the river – until one jump was fatal and locals blew up the rock to avoid such a tragedy reoccurring.

A family-owned boutique vineyard, the vines at Sandihurst are low-yielding but produce grapes with a very distinct character that in turn make very individual wines, including Riesling, Gewürztraminer, Pinot Noir, Chardonnay and Pinot Gris. Their Riesling is more similar to the classical Moselle-style German wine than the usual drier New Zealand style.

To assist with ripening and increased yield, owners Hennie and Celia Bosman have experimented with several types of heat-reflecting ground cover such as glass and mussel shells, with the glass in particular giving the vineyard a colourful character. In the tasting room visitors are most likely to be taken through the tasting of the Sandihurst range by either Hennie or Celia, who are more than happy to personalise the tasting to suit your tastes. The cellar door also has a display of local artists that changes regularly.

Sandihurst Winery

**1320 West Coast Road
West Melton
(near Christchurch)**

Labels **Sandihurst**

Specialisation **Riesling**

Opening hours
Daily 11 am–5 pm

Tasting **$5 for six wines,
refundable on purchase**

Phone **03 347 8269**

Website
www.sandihurstwines.co.nz

Tresillian Estate

45 Johnston Road
West Melton
(near Christchurch)

Labels **Tresillian**

Specialisation **Pinot Noir**
Pinot Gris

Opening hours
Oct–Apr Sat/Sun 11 am–5 pm

Tasting **$5 for five wines,
discounted against
purchase of two bottles**
Phone **03 347 4103**
Website **www.tresillian.co.nz**

A small boutique vineyard of just eight hectares, Tresillian produces hand-crafted wines that include Pinot Noir, Pinot Gris, Sauvignon Blanc and Riesling made only from Canterbury grapes. The vineyard prides itself on being environmentally sustainable. This family-owned winery has recently opened a tiny and intimate tasting room where visitors will be taken through Tresillian's wines with the owners.

Screwcaps and corks

Screwcaps are an alternative wine closure in place of the traditional cork. The use of screwcaps is seen to be a New Zealand initiative in response to winemakers protecting their bottled wine against 'cork taint'. The quality of cork received in New Zealand over the years has been variable to say the least, and it is estimated that in 1986 approximately 15–20% of New Zealand wine was infected with cork taint. As recently as 2005 it was established that 7% of wine in the USA was tainted. As screwcaps provide a tighter seal and can keep out oxygen for a longer period than cork, a wine's overall quality, especially aromatic freshness, is enhanced and its ageing potential is improved.

Akarua Winery

Noted for its award-winning Pinot Noir, from a single estate of 50 hectares in the tough soils above Lake Dunstan, Akarua produces wines that encompass Chardonnay (barrel-fermented and unoaked), Pinot Gris, and a Pinot Noir Rosé, with a Riesling due in the near future. The 2002 Pinot Noir won the Pinot Noir Trophy at the Air New Zealand Wine Awards, and subsequently its Pinot Noir has won Air New Zealand gold medals three years in succession.

Alongside is the very popular Lazy Dog Café and Wine Bar, which has both indoor and outdoor dining in a great courtyard atmosphere and, unusually for a winery restaurant, is open for both lunch and dinner. In addition to wine tasting, Akarua offers winery and vineyard tours by arrangement, and also brews three types of beer on the premises under the Wild Spaniard label.

Cairnmuir Road
Bannockburn
(near Cromwell)

Labels **Akarua**

Specialisation **Pinot Noir**

Opening hours
Mon–Fri 10 am–5 pm
Sat/Sun 11 am–4 pm

Tasting **No charge**
Phone **03 445 0897**
Website **www.akarua.com**

Dessert wines, sweet wines and 'stickies'

Sweet wines are made by ensuring that some 'residual sugar' remains after fermentation is completed. This can be done by harvesting late (e.g. late harvest wines), freezing the grapes to concentrate the sugar (e.g. ice wines) or adding a substance to kill the remaining yeast before fermentation is complete (e.g. adding brandy when making fortified wines such as port).

Amisfield Wine Company

10 Lake Hayes Road
Queenstown

Labels **Amisfield**
Lake Hayes
Arcadia

Specialisation **Pinot Gris**
Riesling
Sauvignon Blanc

Opening hours
Daily 10 am–6 pm,
Bistro Tues–Sun 11.30 am–8 pm

Tasting **$5 for four wines,**
refundable on purchase

Phone **03 442 0556**

Website **www.amisfield.co.nz**

The closest vineyard to Queenstown, Amisfield is a stunning modern winery overlooking Lake Hayes. The dining is sophisticated, both indoor and outdoor, and the Amisfield Bistro won the 2006 Vineyard Restaurant of the Year Award.

All estate-grown and single-vineyard, Amisfield wines come in three distinct ranges. The Amisfield label is reserved for top-of-the-range wines and includes Riesling, Noble Sauvignon, Rosé, Pinot Noir, Pinot Gris and Sauvignon Blanc; it is this range that receives most of Amisfield's accolades. The Lake Hayes label is more fruit-driven and broader with Chardonnay, Pinot Gris, Riesling and Pinot Noir, while Arcadia is reserved solely for the sparkling wine range of Blanc de Noir, Blanc de Blanc and Brut.

Vintage

The vintage is the harvesting of the grapes and hence the wine made from the grapes of that specific harvest, the date of which will be shown on the label. As with any farming enterprise, the vintage can vary considerably from year to year, affected by early frosts, cool summers, autumn rain and many other climatic variations. A good grape harvest is essential for good wines.

Producing only wines from its own Lowburn vineyard located on the 45° South latitude line, this boutique vineyard of just 13 hectares makes Pinot Noir, Pinot Gris, Riesling and Chardonnay. Being very new to the area, Aurum has only just started making wine but already its Riesling has made it into *Cuisine*'s Top 10 New Zealand Rieslings.

The cellar door is a beautiful 1920s worker's cottage lovingly restored with polished floors and a tasteful white-and-yellow, slightly French, colour scheme that matches the very French zinc top. From the porch the view is over the cottage garden towards the grand and imposing Pisa Range. As well as wine tasting and sales, Aurum has local olive oil available for tasting and purchase, plus selected gifts that include lavender cosmetics.

Aurum Wines

140 State Highway 6 Cromwell

Labels **Aurum**

Specialisation **Pinot Noir**
Riesling

Opening hours
Daily 10 am–5 pm

Tasting **No charge**

Phone **03 445 3620**

Website **www.aurumwines.co.nz**

Bannock Brae Estate

212 Cairnmuir Road
Bannockburn
(near Cromwell)

Labels   Bannock Brae
         Goldfields

Specialisation Pinot Noir

Opening hours
Dec–Mar daily 11 am–5 pm,
    other times by appointment

Tasting   No charge
Phone   025 221 0695
Website www.bannockbrae.co.nz

If it is a boutique winery you are looking for, then go no further than this small family-owned vineyard at Bannockburn, just south of Cromwell. The vines were first planted in 1999 but Bannock Brae immediately became a quality Pinot Noir winemaker. Winning golds at the Air New Zealand Wine Awards in 2001 and 2002, Bannock Brae won half the Air New Zealand golds awarded to Central Otago Pinot Noir wine in 2007. *Cuisine* magazine in 2007 has rated their Pinot Noir five star, and also (in 2004) ranked Brannock Brae as top New Zealand Pinot Noir Producer on the basis of their 'Barrel Selection'.

Brannock Brae is a single-estate vineyard of just eight hectares, owned by Crawford Brown and wife Catherine, and while producing only 3000 cases per year, their overriding ethic of quality has clearly paid off. In addition to Pinot Noir the vineyard produces Riesling, which has also won its share of accolades, and which is available only at the cellar door and selected local outlets.

The 'tasting room' is in fact the terrace of the owners' home with a marvellous view east towards the mountains and the Kawarau Gorge. They will happily take you through a wine tasting that in reality is more like a chat with good friends who just like to share the wine they have made.

Overlooking the Bannockburn inlet of Lake Dunstan, and in the distance the Carrick Range from which the winery takes its name, Carrick is a privately owned single-estate vineyard known for Pinot Noir, Riesling, Chardonnay, Pinot Gris and Sauvignon Blanc.

The cellar door and restaurant atmosphere is friendly and relaxed, with a blazing fire in winter and deep comfortable couches. The walls are lined with huge New Zealand works of art that fit comfortably into the open building, taking advantage of its expansive walls and high ceilings. With its marvellous view across the lawn to the mountains beyond, Carrick is open for lunch only and emphasises innovative regional cuisine while at the same time allowing for seasonal availability (all the food is made on the premises). The prices are modest and the menu varied, including for smaller meals or tasting platters that can be enjoyed on the terrace with a glass of wine or a coffee. Glass floor-panels allow a peek into the huge barrel hall below, which easily holds over 300 barrels of maturing wine, and a window in the back wall gives a view into the winery. Visitors are also encouraged to take a walk around the vines adjoining the winery and take a close-up look at the grapes' progress.

Carrick Wines

Cairnmuir Road
Bannockburn
(near Cromwell)

Labels **Carrick**

Specialisation **Pinot Noir**
Riesling

Opening hours
Daily 11 am–5 pm

Tasting **$4, refundable on purchase**

Phone **03 445 3480**

Website **www.carrick.co.nz**

Chard Farm Winery

Chard Farm Road
Off State Highway 6
Gibbston

Labels Chard Farm

Specialisation Pinot Noir
Pinot Gris
Riesling

Opening hours
Mon–Fri 10 am–5 pm
Sat/Sun 11 am–5 pm

Tasting **No charge**
Phone **03 442 6110**

Website **www.chardfarm.co.nz**

Chard Farm is one of New Zealand's most spectacularly sited vineyards. The grapes are planted to the very edge of the high bluffs above the roaring Kawarau River, and steep, rocky, sunburnt hills create a towering backdrop to this winery. The road leading to the vineyard is an experience in itself, and it is hard to believe that this narrow gravel road was the main road through the gorge during the nineteenth century. An added bonus for the vineyard visitor is that the road is too narrow for large tour buses. From the broad sunny terrace in front of the winery, the snow-clad Coronet Peak can be seen in the distance, while across the river is the distinct outline of the rock formation known as the Judge and Jury which gives its name to Chard Farm's Pinot Noir.

The stylish winery is a simple French Country-inspired building, with a unique colouring that blends into the delicate Otago landscape. Inside, the warm and inviting tasting room is lined with historical photos. It is not surprising that this vineyard was top in the 2005 Readers Poll in *Unlimited* magazine for the best New Zealand winery experience.

Dramatic location aside, family-owned Chard Farm produces excellent wines with all their grapes hand-picked and all the processes carried out at the winery in the valley. The range includes award-winning Pinot Noir, Pinot Gris, Riesling, Chardonnay, Rosé and Gewürztraminer.

For the first-time visitor to the Bannockburn area, it comes as a surprise that this dry, barren area can grow any vegetation, let alone some of the best wine grapes in the country. Yet Felton Road produces a range of wines second to none, including Pinot Noir, Riesling, Chardonnay and Vin Gris, a white wine made from Pinot Noir grapes and produced only in certain years when the grapes are large. With three vineyards at Bannockburn totalling 30 hectares, Felton Road produces single-block wines and also blends between the vineyards. All grapes are organically and biodynamically grown and, with quality the priority, great care is taken to handle the fruit with the minimum interference possible. This includes no filtering, and situated on a slope the winery is gravity-fed, allowing the fruit to be handled as gently as possible.

The family-owned winery is housed in a handsome corrugated-iron building sitting on a north-facing slope overlooking the grapes, but the cellar door has rather short opening hours as Felton Road wines are produced only in limited quantities and sell out fast.

Felton Road Wines

Felton Road Bannockburn (near Cromwell)

Labels Felton Road

Specialisation Pinot Noir
Chardonnay
Riesling

Opening hours
Mon–Fri 2 pm–5 pm
  or by appointment

Tasting No charge
Phone 03 445 0885
Website www.feltonroad.co.nz

Gibbston Valley Wines

**State Highway 6
Gibbston Valley
Queenstown**

Labels   Gibbston Valley
          Gold River

Specialisation   Pinot Noir
                  Riesling

Opening hours
Daily 10 am–5 pm
Closed public holidays except
  New Year's Day

Tasting $5 for four wines of the
          winemaker's selection;
          individual charges for
          tasting library wines;
          refundable on purchase
          of three bottles

Phone   03 442 6910

Website   www.gvwines.co.nz

Attracting over 150,000 visitors a year, Gibbston Valley Wines is New Zealand's most popular winery. Unusually for a New Zealand vineyard it exports very little, selling 70% of its annual 20,000 cases through the cellar door. Located in the picturesque Gibbston Valley in the Kawarau Gorge, this winery was the pioneer of grape growing in the area with plantings as early as 1981 and their first commercial vintage in 1987. Their Pinot Noir has won numerous awards over the years, though it was their Gibbston Valley 2005 Riesling that won the Air New Zealand Champion Trophy. Along with Pinot Noir and Riesling, the winery also produces Pinot Gris, oaked and unoaked Chardonnay, late harvest Riesling, a Pinot Noir Rosé and Sauvignon Blanc from Marlborough-sourced grapes.

Despite the sheer number of visitors Gibbston Valley has a surprisingly relaxed atmosphere, with bus tours subtly kept separate from independent visitors. The spacious tasting area, lined with wine awards, adjoins the large courtyard restaurant; as well as offering tastings, it has a wide range of Gibbston Valley vintages available including magnums of Pinot Noir. A large retail area sells wine- and food-related gifts, books, chocolates made with Gibbston Valley wines, local olive oils, preserves and spices. Right next door is the Gibbston Valley Cheese Company which produces boutique varieties from both cow and sheep milk and has a range of cheese for tasting.

The restaurant serves local produce such as lamb, smoked salmon and venison with a Mediterranean flair under the watchful eye of chef Mark Sage, who has been with Gibbston Valley for over 12 years. For such a popular vineyard the food prices are reasonable, and if you are not in the mood for a meal then wine is available by the bottle or glass.

Gibbston Valley's barrel hall is very impressive. Not just a gimmick, it extends 70 metres into rock, keeping maturing wines at such a constant temperature that no climate control is necessary. Tours, which take around 30 minutes, culminate in a wine tasting in the cave of gold medal wines.

Kawarau Estate Vineyard

927 Wanaka Road
Cromwell

Labels Kawarau Estate

Specialisation Pinot Noir
Chardonnay

Opening hours
Boxing Day–end Jan
daily 10 am–5 pm
Nov–Mar (excluding Jan)
Mon–Fri 10 am–5 pm
Apr–Oct
10 am–5 pm but call ahead

Tasting No charge
Phone 03 445 1315

Website
www.kawarauestate.co.nz

Located 10 kilometres north of Cromwell on the road to Wanaka, Kawarau Estate was the first vineyard to be planted on the Pisa Flats in the Lowburn area, now home to several vineyards. This certified organic winemaker takes a long view when creating wines, an approach that has clearly paid off with the Reserve Pinot Noir receiving gold medals six years in a row. Kawarau's other wines are not left behind either, with its Reserve Chardonnay picking up two golds. In addition to these two wines, the 14-hectare single-estate vineyard also makes Sauvignon Blanc and Pinot Gris.

The tasting room at Kawarau, however, is pleasantly modest. Located in a cosy old brick-lined garage warmly decorated with old wine barrels, there is a friendly welcome to match from resident wine expert Jonathan Holdsworth.

Mt Difficulty Wines

Felton Road
Bannockburn
(near Cromwell)

Labels   Mt Difficulty
          Roaring Meg

Specialisation   Pinot Noir
                 Riesling

Opening hours
Daily 10 am–5 pm
Café 12 noon–3 pm

Tasting   No charge, groups by
          appointment
Phone   03 445 3445

Website   www.mtdifficulty.co.nz

There is something immediately appealing about a winery called Mt Difficulty that goes beyond the award-winning wines that this winery produces. At the 2007 World Pinot Noir Conference, the Mt Difficulty 2003 Pinot Noir was acclaimed as top international Pinot Noir, and Mt Difficulty also won the Riesling Trophy at the 2007 Royal Easter Show. The Mt Difficulty label covers the estate-grown, hand-picked wines from Bannockburn, while the Roaring Meg label is for contract-grown fruit though all grapes are processed at the Bannockburn winery.

Equally famous is the stylish winery restaurant and cellar door. Overlooking the Cromwell Basin, the view is second to none and the clean low lines of this building designed by David McBride fit naturally into the landscape. The dining is casual with an uncomplicated cuisine, including platters which can be enjoyed with a glass of wine on the terrace. Be aware, this restaurant is small and very popular, and with only the inside tables able to be booked, reservations are highly recommended.

The oldest vineyard in the Cromwell basin, Olssens first planted vines in 1989 with plantings of Pinot Noir in 1991, and now produce Riesling, Sauvignon Blanc, Pinot Noir, Gewürztraminer and dessert wine. Family-owned and single-estate, Olssens do more than produce award-winning wine. Working in such a delicate environment as Central Otago, Olssens in 2005 won the Ballance Farm Environment Award, and for two years running won the coveted winemakers' award the Bragato Trophy.

Surrounded by Pinot Noir vines, Olssens' cellar door is an old school classroom, beautifully restored with polished wooden floors and a warm colour scheme to match the sunny location. A wide terrace shaded by a wisteria-covered pergola leads out into a beautiful garden that features contemporary outdoor sculpture, a pond and lovely shade trees, just perfect to picnic under though food platters are also available over the summer months. Olssens host 'Music in the Vines' in January, and a sculpture exhibition (by invitation only) on Labour Weekend.

Olssens

**306 Felton Road
Bannockburn
(near Cromwell)**

Labels **Olssens**

Specialisation **Pinot Noir
Riesling**

Opening hours
**Labour Weekend–Queen's
Birthday**
  daily 10 am–5 pm
Rest of year
  Mon–Fri 11 am–4 pm

Tasting **No charge**
Phone **03 445 1716**
Website **www.olssens.co.nz**

P. Reynolds

Peregrine Wines

Kawarau Gorge Road
Gibbston Valley
Queenstown

Labels Peregrine
        Saddleback
        Wentworth
        Pinnacles

Specialisation Pinot Noir
                Pinot Gris
                Riesling

Opening hours
Daily 10 am–5 pm

Tasting No charge

Phone 03 442 4000

Website
www.peregrinewines.co.nz

While Peregrine is best known for its stunningly modern winery located in the Kawarau Gorge, the winery has two of Central Otago's oldest stone buildings: an old shearing shed and a stone cottage both dating from the mid-nineteenth century. Rather than replicate the old, the new barrel hall and tasting room are located under a massive shimmering metallic wing, which at a glance does not reveal the beauty underground. Strolling into the winery around the ponds designed to attract native birds, it is in fact quite easy to miss the entrance to the cellar door partially hidden underground, as it has been carefully designed both to keep the maturing wine cool and to refrain from imposing too much on the landscape. With back-lit bottles of wine, a wall of glass between the tasting room and the barrel hall, and severe minimalist lines, the underground facility is immediately appealing.

But Peregrine is more than just stylish buildings, old or new. Sourcing grapes from 12 Central Otago vineyards, the winery blends between sites to achieve the right balance in its wines. Its Pinot Noir is the most consistently awarded Pinot Noir in New Zealand. Producing Pinot Noir, Pinot Gris, Riesling, Sauvignon Blanc, Gewürztraminer and Chardonnay, Peregrine is also well known for the summer concerts held in the vineyard in February and March, and an outdoor fashion parade of innovative new Otago clothing labels (details on the website).

Nick Mills/Rippon Vineyard and Winery

One of the most spectacular and most photographed vineyards in the country, Rippon sits on a sloping site above Lake Wanaka with the most marvellous vista across the lake to the magnificent Southern Alps to the west, especially attractive in autumn when the yellowing leaves of the vines contrast with the bright blue of the lake. Rippon doesn't have a café but is a great place to bring a picnic. The tasting room is modest and friendly, and also accessible by a pleasant 45-minute walk along the lake from Wanaka township.

Throughout the 1970s, despite the cynics, Rippon owners Lois and Rolfe Mills experimented with a variety of grape types at Wanaka before planting their first commercial vines in 1981. Despite many viticultural dead-ends, Rippon now produces Riesling, Pinot Noir, Gewürztraminer and Sauvignon Blanc as well as two very unusual wines, a Gamay-based Rosé, and Osteiner, a white wine.

Rippon is also well known for its innovative 'golf cross' course, a fast running game inspired by golf and using an oval-shaped golf ball. Equally famous is the annual Rippon Music Festival, held on the first weekend of February, around Waitangi Day. Featuring an impressive line-up of contemporary New Zealand music, the 12-hour festival is limited to 5000 people and tickets sell out months beforehand (see the website for details).

Rippon Vineyard and Winery

246 Mt Aspiring Road Wanaka

Labels Rippon

Specialisation Riesling
Pinot Noir

Opening hours
Dec–Apr
Daily 11 am–5 pm
July–Nov
Daily 1.30 pm–4 pm
Closed May/June unless by appointment

Tasting No charge
Phone 03 443 8084
Website www.rippon.co.nz

Suellen Boag

Rockburn Wines

Cnr Gair Ave and
McNulty Road
Cromwell

Labels Rockburn

Specialisation Pinot Noir

___

Opening hours
Labour Weekend–Easter
  daily 10 am–5 pm
Rest of year
  Mon–Fri 11 am–4 pm

Tasting No charge
Phone 03 445 0555

Website www.rockburn.co.nz

___

Like several Cromwell wineries, Rockburn is located in an industrial area of Cromwell, but manages to rise above the ordinary with its industrial chic style. Winner of the 2004 Winestate Wine of the Year for its 2002 Pinot Noir, Rockburn blends its wine between two distinctly different vineyards, creating unique wines that balance integrity with elegance. In addition to Pinot Noir, the winery makes Gewürztraminer, Chardonnay, Sauvignon Blanc, Pinot Gris and Riesling. From the sparse lines of the tasting room there is a grand view towards Mt Difficulty and the Pisa Range, while a large picture window allows a more personal view into the heart of the working winery.

Producing its first vintage in 1987, William Hill is a family-owned vineyard between Alexandra and Clyde, and all of its wines are produced from grapes grown in the Alexandra area. Their select vintages are bottled under the William Hill label, while their main label Shaky Bridge produces Gewürztraminer that is recognised as one of the best from Central Otago. With over 40 hectares under grapes, all processes are carried out at the winery producing Pinot Noir, Riesling, Chardonnay and Pinot Gris in addition to the Gewürztraminer. Wine writer Jancis Robinson has rated the William Hill Pinot Noir as one of the top five from New Zealand.

The winery has two outlets for tasting wine: at the winery itself in a small and intimate tasting room beautifully constructed of stone quarried from Tarras, and at the Shaky Bridge Café just over the Manuherikia River from central Alexandra. Some select vintages are only available locally.

William Hill Winery

Dunstan Road
Alexandra

Labels William Hill
        Shaky Bridge

Specialisation Pinot Noir
                Gewürztraminer

Opening hours
Labour Weekend–Easter
 daily 10 am–4.30 pm

Tasting No charge

Phone 03 448 8346

Website www.williamhill.co.nz

Wooing Tree Vineyard

7 Westmoreland Place Cromwell

Labels Wooing Tree

Specialisation Pinot Noir
Rosé

Opening hours
Daily 10 am–5 pm (may vary in
winter so phone ahead)

Tasting Casual visitors no charge,
small charge for groups

Phone 03 445 4142

Website www.wooingtree.co.nz

This winery will have immediate appeal for the romantically inclined. The vineyard takes its name from an 80-year-old pine tree located in the heart of the grapes that has long been a destination for the district's courting couples. So strong was local affection for this one tree that the owners not only spared it the axe when clearing the area for grapes, but also decided to name the vineyard after the tree, and use the tree on their label. Today the tree is still a popular spot for couples to pop that all-important question, renew wedding vows, celebrate a special anniversary or just picnic quietly in its shade. One can imagine the tree attracting quite a crowd on Valentine's Day . . . but then, it *is* a big tree.

However, Wooing Tree is about wine as much as romance, and produces Chardonnay, Pinot Noir, Rosé and the unusual wine Blondie. This is a white wine made from Pinot Noir but with a taste closer to Pinot Gris or Viognier than to the red wine. Its first wine, the 2005 Pinot Noir, won the 2006 Air New Zealand Trophy and its 2006 Rosé won the trophy at the Royal Easter Show. Family-owned and family-run, Wooing Tree is a single-estate vineyard; it opened the cellar door in 2006. Located in the heart of the grape vines, the tasting room and small bar offers cheese and platters to accompany the wines, and in colder weather a toasty open fire keeps away any winter chills. Just handy outside is a small fenced playground for the young ones, complete with sandpit and slide.